Eat the Norway

Thank you Michael !

Love

Anne-Marie

AASE STRØMSTAD

Eat the Norway

Traditional Dishes and Specialities from Norwegian Cooking

TRANSLATED BY MARY LEE NIELSEN

ASCHEHOUG · OSLO 1985

Contents

© H. Aschehoug & Co. (W. Nygaard) 1984
Second printing 1985
Translated from the Norwegian manuscript
Cover photo: Bjørn Winsnes
Other photos (t – top, b – bottom): Bokgruppen
i Malmö (56-t, 58-t), Frionor Norsk Frossen-
fisk A/L (36-b), A/S Hjemmet (57-b), Norske
Meieriers Salgssentral (96-b), Opplysnings-
kontoret for kjøtt (56-b, 57-t), Opplysnings-
utvalget for Fisk (37, 38), Ragge Strand (17-b,
35, 36-t, 55-t, 58-b, 75-b, 76-t, 77-t, 95), Bengt
Wilson A/S (17-t, 18-t, 18-b, 75-t, 76-b, 77-b,
78, 96-t)
End paper: A dangerous road beneath Fillefjell,
in Galdane, Borgund. Copper-plate engraving
from Erik Pontoppidan's description of Norway (1752–1753)
Photosetting: Heien Fotosats, Spydeberg
Color printing: Aske Trykkeri A.S., Stavanger
Text printing: Gjøvik Trykkeri A.s., Gjøvik
Binding: A/S Bokbind, Oslo
Printed in Norway

ISBN 82-03-11407-5

Cover photo:
Saddle of reindeer, served with brussels sprouts, potatoes, boiled apples
filled with jelly, and cream gravy, is a
meal for a very special occasion
(recipe on page 53).

Foreword

In this little book I have collected a number of Norwegian recipes – dishes the tourist may sample in hotels and restaurants, but also dishes that never find their way to the larger dining establishments – fare served in the typical Norwegian home – everyday food and food for special occasions. Rarely does the ordinary tourist have the opportunity to taste these dishes, though he may have heard them mentioned if the conversation turned to that most interesting topic – food.

Norwegian food is reputed to be dull – unvaried and flavorless. Let us rather call it honest. It is not seasoned like more exotic foods but is boiled or fried, and served with simple garnishes.

Norwegian cuisine has one advantage that is rare in the world today – fresh, untainted raw materials are still widely available. It is true that we, too, feel the disturbing threat of pollution, but we can safely eat fish fresh from the sea, game and berries from our forests and mountains. There is strict control of the use of poisonous sprays in Norway, so that fruits and vegetables may be eaten raw. Our flour is unbleached and without additives. Our milk, butter and cheese are pure and untreated, retaining their fresh, natural flavor.

I hope that you, as a tourist in Norway, will enjoy this freshness to the full and will have occasion to taste the best of the good food we serve our guests. This little book may then help you recreate your favorite dishes when you return to your own country.

Oslo, May 1984

Aase Strømstad

Norwegian Food and Culinary Traditions

A country's culture and culinary traditions are influenced by its natural resources. Thus it has been and still is throughout most of the world – in our country, also.

When men lived as nomads they depended for food on fish from lakes, rivers and the sea. They hunted game in the woods and mountains and gathered wild berries and plants.

Later, when they settled down and began to cultivate the soil, grain became their most important source of nourishment. Meat and fish were served less often. We read in old accounts that until the middle of the last century, porridge was eaten twice or even three times daily in Norway.

Ordinary porridge was made of coarsely ground grains and water, or skimmed milk, and everyone ate it from the same large wooden bowl. On special occasions, however, fine-ground flour and heavy cream were used to make a holiday treat, a refinement of which is *rømmegrøt*, or sour cream pudding, considered a delicacy to this day.

Norway's severe climate made it difficult to grow grain. In cold, wet summers the crop did not mature, and the poor quality grain spoiled easily in storage. The best way to preserve such grain was to bake it into *flatbrød*. This thin, unleavened bread is known to have been eaten in Norway at least as early as 1300 A.D. The large, dry wafers kept for months. Great quantities were baked twice a year and stacked in a dry *stabbur*, or store-house. Like porridge, *flatbrød* was made of coarse flour for everyday, fine flour for special occasions. Yeasted bread as we now know it, was rare in Norway until the seventeenth century.

Lefse and cakes were only used for festive meals and were made of the finest ground and sifted flour. They were thin and often elaborately made. The first cakes we know of were baked on special irons over the open fire. These irons were beautifully decorated – much as the *krumkake* and *goro* irons still in use today.

Fish has always been an important resource in Norway. Along the coast, where the fisherman caught more than his family could consume, the surplus was sold to provide money for other essentials. Fish that could not be eaten fresh was dried and salted. It is believed that Norwegians have been drying fish for over 1000 years.

Clipfish *(klippfisk)* – fish split, salted and dried in the sun, on rocky ledges – is a more recent method of preserving fish that became possible only after salt came to Norway. From that time, too, we hear of salted herring – a food that assumed a position second only to grain as a source of nourishment. It was not uncommon to have salted herring on the table for at least one meal every day. It was eaten right from the salt tub, without further ado. The flavorful and varied dishes of salted herring that we enjoy today are from more modern kitchens.

Far from the coast, in the interior of the country, fresh water fish was predominant. Salmon, trout, char, pike, perch and other fish were eaten daily. Here, too, it was necessary to find ways of preserving the surplus. Thus, for example, *rakefisk* – fermented fish – was developed.

Cattle raising has also played an important role in Norwegian food production, providing meat, milk, butter and cheese. Hunting in the woods and mountains enriched the frugal diet with small game such as ptarmigan, grouse and hare; larger game like moose, reindeer and deer.

Both slaughtering and hunting took place in the fall. Only then could one enjoy fresh meat. This is certainly one of the reasons that Christmas has always been a very special holiday for Norwegians, giving us many of our finest culinary traditions. At Christmas one could eat fresh meat to one's heart's content.

For the rest of the year one had to make do with salted, dried and cured meat – food that ironically is considered party fare today, providing variation in the modern diet.

Milk and cream were soured, churned to butter, or curdled for cheese. In this way milk, too, could be preserved and enjoyed throughout the spring season when cows gave little milk.

Thus many dishes that are considered culinary specialties in today's Norway have their origin in the need to preserve surplus produce from the farm, the sea, the woods and the mountains.

Preparation of the raw ingredients was simple. Food was usually boiled – everything in a single iron pot that hung above the hearth. Meat and fish were often roasted over the flames or coals, and bread was baked on large flagstones placed over the fire. Seasonings were used sparingly. Herbs and berries were generally utilized medicinally, in magic potions to keep away evil spirits, or in love potions.

Although herbs and seasonings are more commonly used today, Norwegian cuisine is still characterized by plain, uncomplicated cooking. We still prefer those dishes where the flavor of the main ingredient is dominant.

While Norwegian food is simply prepared, great importance is attached to its presentation. It is nicely presented, attractively arranged and garnished. Even everyday meals are often served on tables carefully laid with tablecloth, flowers and candles.

Hearty soups

Supper

In many countries dinner always begins with soup. This is rarely the case in Norway where soup as a first course belongs to the more important occasions – confirmations, weddings and special birthday celebrations.

Norwegian soups are generally so filling that they constitute the main course at everyday meals. Soups such as fish soup, pea soup and others are so laden with vegetables, fish and meat that they are a meal in themselves. «Flatbrød», that thin, crisp, unleavened bread that is found nowhere else in the world, is the traditional accompaniment to soup, though in modern homes bread is more and more apt to take its place.

When soup is served as the main course it is customarily followed by a rich dessert. Thus pea soup is always succeeded by thin Norwegian pancakes rolled around a filling of blueberries or jam. French toast, bread puddings or various apple desserts are also often served with a soup dinner.

Green Soup

Grønn suppe

In early spring this soup is made from wild greens such as nettles and carraway. Later, garden greens like spinach and kale may be substituted.

Ingredients
1 liter/1 qt fresh greens
  (see above), washed
1 liter/ 1 qt meat or vegetable stock
2 1/2 Tb flour
salt
1/4 tsp nutmeg
4–6 Tb cream

Remove coarse stems from the green leaves. Wash leaves well. Steam them tightly covered in a little water for 5–10 minutes. Drain. Chop leaves fine or run them in the blender. Stir the flour into the cold stock and bring to a boil stirring constantly. Add the greens and season to taste with salt and nutmeg. Bring to a boil.

For a milder flavor add cream just before serving. If a tangier taste of greens is preferred omit the cream. Serve warm with half a hard-boiled egg or a few croutons in each dish.

Cauliflower Soup

Blomkålsuppe

This is traditionally a festive soup that is served as a first course on special occasions and at formal dinners. Asparagus soup is made in the same way.

Ingredients
500 g/1 lb cauliflower
soup greens*
1 liter/1 qt water
2 tsp salt
2 Tb butter or margarine
2 Tb flour
1 egg yolk
3–4 Tb cream
3 Tb sherry

Clean the cauliflower and divide it into florets. Cut the stem into small pieces.

Boil cauliflower stem with soup greens in lightly salted water. When the vegetables are tender add the florets and boil 2–3 minutes until barely done. Remove the florets and puré stems and soup greens with

* A few leaves of parsley, celery, parsnip or other flavorful vegetable tops are tied in the folded green ends of a leek and cooked with the soup for flavor.

liquid. Add water or stock to make 1 ½ liter/ 1 ½ qt strained liquid in all.

Melt butter, stir in flour and add stock. Mix well and boil for 5–10 minutes.

Whisk egg yolk and cream together and stir them into the soup. Add salt and sherry to taste. Add cauliflower florets and serve piping hot.

Pea Soup

Ertesuppe

The best pea soup is made from the bone of a cured ham or mutton. Soak bones in cold water for 6–8 hours so the soup will not be too salty.

This is a very filling soup that is served as a main course. It is traditionally followed by Norwegian pancakes for dessert.

Ingredients
250 g/ ½ lb dried yellow peas
soup greens (see footnote page 9)
1 ½–2 liters/1½–2 qt water
bone of a cured ham or mutton
1 thick slice of rutabaga
2 carrots
2–3 potatoes
1 large onion

Soak peas overnight in sufficient water to cover them. Drain. Add fresh water, 1 ½–2 qt, and bring to a boil. Add soup greens and ham or mutton bone and simmer until peas are cooked, 1 ½–2 hours.

Remove the soup greens and the bone. Taste the soup. Add water if it is too salty.

Cube vegetables and boil them tender in the soup.

Serve pea soup piping hot and sprinkle with thyme if desired. *Flatbrød* usually accompanies pea soup.

Vegetable Soup

Betasuppe (Photo on page 17)

This soup differs from pea soup in the addition of whole barley kernels and cubed meat.

Ingredients
4 Tb whole barley
100 g/3 oz/½ cup dried yellow peas
1 ½ liter/1 ½ qt cold water
250 g/½ lb salted lamb or ham
1 thick slice rutabaga
2–3 carrots
2–3 potatoes
1 large onion
parsley

Soak peas and barley over night. Drain. Add fresh water and boil peas and barley about 1 ½ hours. Cube the meat and add it to the soup. Simmer about ½ hour and add cubed vegetables and potatoes.

Continue to simmer the soup until everything is done, approximately 15–20 minutes. Sprinkle chopped parsley over soup and serve with *flatbrød*.

Fish Soup from Bergen

Bergensk fiskesuppe

In the past Bergen was an important port for the fishing trade. Today its picturesque fish market is worth a visit. Although this recipe originates in Bergen it is known and used throughout the country. It is best when made from young pollack, but any fish that gives a tasty stock, such as mackerel, flounder or perch, may be used.

Ingredients
fish trimmings (head, tail, bones and skin)
*   of 1 ½ kg/3 lb fish*
1 ½ liter/1 ½ qt water
2 ½ dl/1 cup milk
5 Tb flour
2 carrots
1 parsley root or parsnip
1 dl/½ cup light sour cream
chives

Rinse fish trimmings well removing all traces of blood. Put trimmings in a pan and cover with cold water. Bring to boil and skim. Lower heat and let the stock simmer for 20 minutes. Longer cooking gives fish stock a gluey flavor. Strain the stock.

Whisk flour smooth in the cold milk and beat it into the boiling stock.

Clean carrots and parsley root and cut them in thin slices. Boil them a few minutes in lightly salted water, using as little water as possible. Add the vegetables and their liquid to the soup. Season to taste. Stir sour cream into soup just before serving and sprinkle with chives. Serve with pumpkin or watermelon pickle and *flatbrød*.

Seafood Chowder

Sørlandssuppe

The amateur fisherman will particularly like this recipe. Here he may combine the many too-small-to-eat fish in his catch to make a culinary treat. Crabs, clams, mussels and shrimp can all go into the pot.

Ingredients
2–3 kg/4–6 lb small fish such as cod,
  pollack, flounder, perch etc.
2 liter/2 qt water
1 onion

The Soup
2 Tb butter
1 onion
2 stalks of celery
2 carrots
2 leeks
3 bay leaves
1 tsp thyme
juice of ½ lemon
salt and pepper
fish (see above)
shrimp
shellfish
small crabs

Add water and onion to heads and tails of fish. Bring to a boil. Simmer 20 minutes. Strain stock.

Chop onion, cut celery, carrots and leeks in small pieces. Sauté lightly in butter without browning. Add vegetables to stock with bay leaves, thyme and lemon juice. Bring to a boil and simmer about 5 minutes. Season to taste. Add fish in bite-size pieces, shrimp, crabs and shellfish. Simmer until done, about 5 minutes. Serve piping hot with French bread.

Meat Soup

Kjøttsuppe (photo on page 17)

A popular soup for cold weather, often served as an accompaniment to boiled meat with onion sauce (see page 44).

Ingredients
1 ½ liter/1 ½ qt meat stock
1–2 carrots
1 parsley root or parsnip
½ celeriac or 2 stalks of celery
¼ head of cabbage
salt and pepper
chopped parsley

Dumplings
4 Tb butter or margarine
6 Tb water
6 Tb flour
1 large egg
1 tsp sugar
¼ tsp salt
½ tsp cardamom

Cube all vegetables and boil in the stock until tender. Season to taste.

Dumplings: Bring butter and water to a boil, add flour all at once and stir quickly until mixture no longer clings to sides of bowl. Add egg, salt, sugar and cardamon. Shape into small balls with a teaspoon and drop into lightly salted boiling water for about 10 minutes. Add dumplings to soup before serving.

Sprinkle soup with parsley and serve with *flatbrød*.

Hogback Soup

Svineryggsuppe

This soup is usually eaten at Christmas time when one is apt to have left-over stock from boiling the Christmas ham and other seasonal meats.

Ingredients

2 Tb margarine or bacon fat
4 Tb flour
1 liter/1 qt stock from a boiled ham,
   sausages etc.
1 carrot
1 apple
8–10 pitted prunes
salt
1–2 tsp vinegar
1–2 tsp sugar

Brown fat and flour together to the color of milk chocolate. Add stock and boil soup at least 10 minutes.

Cut carrot in thin slices and apple into small wedges. Add to soup with prunes and simmer.

Season to taste with salt, pepper, vinegar and sugar. The soup should have a fresh sweet-and-sour flavor.

Dumplings (see page 11) may be served in the soup.

Hogback soup is served in small soup bowls as a first course.

Jenny Lind Soup

Jenny Lind-suppe

For some unknown reason this soup bears the name of the famous Swedish singer. In spite of its name the soup is as Norwegian as can be.

Ingredients

1 liter/1 qt meat or vegetable stock
2 ½ Tb tapioca
1 carrot
1 slice of celeriac or 1 stalk of celery
2 egg yolks
½ tsp salt
3–4 Tb cream

Boil tapioca in stock until soft. Cube vegetables and cook them tender in the soup.

Beat egg yolks, salt and cream together and stir them into the soup. Do not let the soup boil after the egg and cream have been added or it will separate.

Serve as a first course.

Trønder Chowder

Trøndersodd

Sodd is still party food in Trøndelag as in some other parts of the country. In some areas, meat, vegetables and potatoes are served as a side dish, in others boiled potatoes are added to the soup at the table. In still other areas it is served as simply as described below.

Ingredients

½ kg/1 lb lamb, for example the shoulder
1 ½ liter/1 ½ qt water
1 ½ tsp salt
½ tsp whole peppercorns
1 piece whole ginger
1 leek
1 carrot
1 parsley root or parsnip
chopped parsley

Chowder dumplings

250 g/½ lb raw lamb, trimmed
1 tsp salt
½ Tb potato flour
2 ½–3 dl/1 cup light cream
nutmeg

Add meat to boiling water. Bring to a boil again and skim carefully. Add salt, pepper, ginger and the green ends of the leeks. Simmer covered over low heat until meat is tender, abbout 1 ½ hours.

Add whole carrot and parsley root to soup pot about 20 minutes before it is done.

Cut meat and vegetables into cubes. Slice thickly the white part of the leek.

Strain stock and pour into a clean pan. Add meat and vegetables to soup with dumplings and heat thoroughly.

Chowder dumplings: Grind the meat 4–5 times, adding salt and potato flour the last two times. Add cream and season with nutmeg. Shape into small balls with a teaspoon and simmer them 15 minutes in lightly salted water.

Serve soup piping hot sprinkled with parsley and accompanied by *flatbrød*.

Delicious Fish Dishes

Fisk

About 200 different kinds of fish live in the waters off Norway's coast. Although all are edible, few may be found at the fish market or on the Norwegian table. Still, the closer one comes to the sea, the greater the variety of fish that is eaten.

Cod, pollack, whiting, haddock, Norway haddock, several varieties of flounder, halibut, herring, mackerel, salmon, trout, char, powan, pike, perch and eel are commonly eaten. In recent years Norwegians have become more and more aware of the fact that what we often call «un-fish» are not only edible but truly delicious. Foremost among these «new» discoveries are monkfish and wolffish, but garfish, dogfish and lumpfish, as well as the fresh water fish, pike perch, are also increasingly popular.

Most Norwegians are extremely discriminating about their seafood. They insist on top quality and demand absolute freshness. Perhaps this is one of the reasons that we show little originality in the preparation of fish. We prefer it boiled or fried with simple garnishes that do not smother the delicate fish flavor.

Norwegians, unlike the people of many other countries, eat a great deal of salt fish. We also relish the liver and roe of several varieties of fish. Fish pudding, fish balls and fish cakes as well as many other fish dishes are daily fare. In our grandmothers' day no formal dinner was complete without the hostess' best homemade fish pudding with shrimp sauce as one of the courses. In many homes fish pudding is still eaten every year on the second day of Christmas – a welcome and wholesome change from the rich and fatty foods served during the Christmas season.

Poached Cod

Avkokt torsk (photo on page 18)

In Norwegian it's «a gentleman's dish», in English, «a dish fit for a king». In other words, a dish to satisfy even the most particular palate. A perfect result can only be attained with absolutely fresh fish – «live», if possible. Then, the fish slices «curl» on the platter and have a characteristically nutty flavor. The accessories to poached cod are simplicity itself – boiled potatoes (preferably the oval, yellow-fleshed Norwegian «mandel», or «almond», potatoes), melted butter – and red wine.

Ingredients
1 whole cod, 2 ½–3 kg/5–6 lb
water to cover
Allow 3–4 Tb salt and 1–2 tsp vinegar for
each liter/qt

Clean fish and remove entrails. Wash well in cold water, being sure to leave no traces of blood. If possible, eviscerate the fish «in the round», without splitting the belly, as this gives more attractive slices. To do this cut a small incision just below the anal opening, severing the intestinal connection. Loosen the gills close to the neckbone and grasp them firmly. Draw the gills, together with the entrails, out of the neck opening, being careful not to pierce the gall bladder.

Cut the fish in 2 cm/1 inch slices and place them in cold, preferably running, water, a precaution that retains the firmness and whiteness of the flesh.

Fill a pan with sufficient water to cover the fish and bring it to a boil. Add salt and vinegar and bring to boil again. Add fish slices to the boiling water and lower heat to just below the simmering point. The fish must *not* boil. Remove fish after 5 minutes or when the flesh loosens easily from the bone. Place on a warm platter and serve at once on heated plates.

The cod head is considered a great delicacy. It is poached alone for 10–15 minutes, according to size. Tradition dictates that the cod head be served to the head of the family.

Liver: The cod liver is also a delicacy and is served with the fish. It is sometimes infected with small parasites that are attached to the membrane enclosing the liver. Remove the membrane carefully and the parasites will follow. Soak the liver in cold water about 1 hour.

In a small pan bring to a boil: 1 dl/½ cup water, 1 tsp salt, 4–5 whole peppercorns, 1 bay leaf and 1 tsp vinegar. Add the liver, being sure that it is completely covered by the liquid, and simmer for about 10 minutes. Serve the liver in the cooking juices. *Flatbrød* is the traditional accompaniment. In many places the liver is cooled in the cooking juices and eaten cold on bread.

Coalfish, American Pollack, Saithe, Rock Salmon: All four names seem to be used for the fish known to Norwegians as *sei.* To avoid confusion I shall refer to it as coalfish. Coalfish is a member of the cod family but has a coarser, grayish flesh. Large coalfish is prepared and served in the same way as cod. Young coalfish is generally used in soup (see page 10).

Prince Fish

Prinsefisk

It is said that this dish was first served in the last century to a Swedish prince visiting Bergen, Norway's second largest city.

Ingredients
¾ kg/2 lb cod fillets
2 tsp salt
2 small lobsters
1 can of asparagus tips
4–8 pastry squares

Sauce
2 Tb butter
3 Tb flour
3 dl/1 cup + 4 Tb/1 ¼ cup cream
3 dl/1 cup + 4 Tb/1 ¼ cup veal stock
3 Tb sherry
salt
white pepper

Place fish fillets in a greased pan. Sprinkle with salt and pepper and pour 1 cup of water over. Steam the fish carefully for 7–10 minutes.

Make white sauce of ingredients above.

Arrange the fish on a warm platter, pour sauce over and garnish with lobster meat, asparagus tops and pastry squares.

Fishball

Fiskeball

This dish originates in northern Vestlandet. It may be made of either fresh or salted fish. Those who are not used to Fishball usually prefer the fresh.

Ingredients
500 g/1 lb raw haddock
500 g/1 lb raw potatoes
2 onions
6–8 Tb barley flour
2 tsp salt
¼ tsp pepper

Poaching Stock
2 liter/2 qt water
1 small salted mutton bone
2 carrots
1 slice kohlrabi or turnip
1 leek
1 tsp thyme

Finely chop or grind the cleaned fish, potatoes and onion together. Knead in flour, salt and pepper, and shape into balls about the size of a tennis ball.

Put all ingredients for stock in a pan and boil for 20 minutes.

Lower the fishballs into the boiling stock and simmer about 15–20 minutes. Test one ball to see if it is cooked through. Serve fishball with boiled salt pork (optional), melted butter and boiled vegetables. Sprinkle with lots of chopped parsley and eat with *flatbrød*.

Poached Salmon and Trout

Kokt laks og ørret

In recent years fish hatcheries have become common along the Norwegian coast. This has made it possible for us to buy salmon and trout – often termed «noble fish» – for a reasonable price all year round. Richer in flavor and color, however, free-swimming salmon and trout are still rated higher than their captive cousins. Salmon fishing in the rapid rivers of Western and Northern Norway is a popular sport that attracts English and American fishermen, as well as Norwegian. In the last century, many Englishmen came to Norway to fish, often building homes and returning year after year.

Ingredients
About 1 kg/2 lb salmon or trout
Allow for each liter/qt of water:
3 Tb salt
1 Tb vinegar
3–4 whole peppercorns
1 stalk of parsley
1 bay leaf

Clean the fish and cut it into 2 cm/1 inch thick slices. Bring the water, with seasonings added, to a boil and simmer about 10 minutes.
   Place the fish slices into the poaching water and lower heat. Poach fish about 8–10 minutes, until the flesh loosens easily from the bone.
   Serve fish warm with boiled potatoes, cucumber salad (see page 67) and Sandefjord butter.

Sandefjord Butter: Boil about ¼ liter/1 cup heavy cream until it is reduced by half. Stir in about 125 g/4 oz/½ cup butter. Season to taste with the grated peel of ½ lemon.

Halibut, monkfish and wolffish may be prepared and served in the same way.

Whole Poached Salmon and Trout

Helkokt laks og ørret

Whole poached salmon and trout may be served warm or cold. When warm they are accompanied by melted butter, Sandefjord butter (see this page), or white wine sauce. Cold, they are eaten with horseradish cream. Boiled potatoes and cucumber salad are traditional accessories to both warm and cold fish.

Ingredients
1 salmon or trout, about 2 kg/4 ½ lb
1 bunch of parsley
juice of ½ lemon
1 Tb salt for every 1 liter/1 qt of water
*   or 1 kg/2 lb fish*

The fish may be poached in water in a poaching kettle or baked in the oven.
   Clean and rinse the fish. Rub it inside and out with lemon juice and put parsley stalks in the belly.

Poached in water: Heat water to about 70 °C/160 °F. Add salt and lower the whole fish into the kettle. Let the fish simmer slowly – it must not boil – for about 30–40 minutes. The fish is done when the dorsal fin may be pulled out easily.
   Cool the fish in the poaching water if it is to be eaten cold.

Baked in the oven: Heat oven to 200 °C/390 °F. Pour a large cup of water into the roasting pan. Rub the fish with salt and lay it in the pan. Cover the pan with aluminum foil, tightly sealed around the edges of the pan. Bake the fish in the oven about 30–40 minutes or until the dorsal fin is easily pulled out.
   If the fish is to be eaten cold, cool it in the pan with the foil over.

Horseradish cream: Whip stiff about 2 ½ dl/1 cup/1 cup heavy cream or sour cream. Add about 2 Tb horseradish, 1 tsp vinegar and 1–2 tsp sugar.

Fried Salmon

Ristet laks (photo on page 18)

In the northern part of Norway and in areas where salmon is found in great quantity, salmon slices are often served lightly fried for the sake of variation. Ordinarily the fish is pan-fried in butter, but for a flavorful difference it may also be broiled.

Ingredients
*4 slices of salmon or trout about
  175 g/6 oz each
2 tsp salt
½ tsp white pepper
4 Tb butter for frying*

Rub fish slices with salt and pepper and fry them golden brown on both sides. Allow 2–3 minutes for each side. Serve salmon slices with boiled potatoes, lettuce and horseradish cream or remoulade.

Remoulade
*2 dl/²/₃ cup/³/₄ cup mayonnaise
6 Tb heavy cream or sour cream
1 Tb capers
1–2 Tb chopped pickle
1 Tb lemon juice
1–2 Tb chopped parsley*

Whip cream lightly and mix it with the mayonnaise. Add the remaining ingredients.
   Halibut, monkfish and wolffish may be prepared in the same way.

Mountain Trout or Char in Sour Cream Sauce

Fjellørret eller røye i rømmesaus

Mountain trout, found in mountain streams throughout Norway, is consider-

ably smaller than hatchery fish or sea trout and has a more pronounced flavor.

Ingredients
*4 mountain trout or char, about
  300–400 g/10–13 oz each
1 Tb salt
4–5 Tb butter for frying
2 dl/²/₃ cup/³/₄ cup sour cream
2 dl/²/₃ cup/³/₄ cup water
1 liter/1 qt fresh chanterelle or
  other mushrooms*

Clean the fish and cut off fins. Rub the inside with salt and brown fish on both sides in butter.
   Add sour cream and water to pan drippings and let the fish simmer in the sauce for about 10 minutes.
   Clean the mushrooms and brown them separately.
   Arrange the fish on a warm platter, pour the sauce over and put the mushrooms on top. Serve with boiled potatoes.

Mackerel may be prepared in the same way but is served without the mushrooms.

Mountain Trout or Char Baked in the Coals

Ørret eller røye på glør

Fish that is wrapped in aluminum foil and baked in the coals of a fire has a particularly strong, fine flavor. This is a popular way for the amateur fisherman to prepare his catch.

Page 17
Top: Vegetable soup is a nourishing soup that is served as the main course at dinner (recipe on page 10).

Bottom: Boiled beef with onion sauce (recipe on page 44) and meat soup with vegetables (recipe on page 11) are filling winter dishes.

16

Ingredients

4 servings of fish, about
  250 g/½ lb per serving
2 tsp salt

Clean and rinse the fish and rub it with salt. Wrap each serving in aluminum foil and place the packages in the coals of a fire. The fish is ready to serve in about 15 minutes. The skin will stick to the foil when the package is opened. Fish prepared in this way is tasty and succulent.

Pickled Mackerel

Syltet makrell

Eaten cold, this is a popular summer dish. Serve with new potatoes, sprinkled with parsley, and cucumber salad.

Ingredients

about 1 kg/2 lb mackerel
1 liter/1 qt water
1 Tb salt
1 Tb vinegar
8 whole peppercorns
1 bay leaf

Clean fish and cut it in slices 5 cm/2 inches thick. Boil the water, vinegar and seasonings about 10 minutes. Add fish slices and poach them for 7–10 minutes.

Cool fish in the vinegar mixture. The fish may be kept refrigerated for a couple of days.

Page 18

Top: Norwegian tradition prescribes a good red wine with poached cod (recipe on page 13).

Bottom: Thick salmon slices may be prepared under the broiler or fried in butter in a frying pan (recipe on page 16). It may be served with stirred butter flavored with anchovy, as shown here, or with remoulade or horseradish cream.

Serve pickled mackerel with potatoes, cucumber salad (see page 67) and horseradish cream (see page 16).

Fried Fillet of Coalfish

Seibiff

A popular dish for everyday meals all over Norway. It may even be purchased frozen, already fried. Be sure to serve it with plenty of fried onions.

Ingredients

¾ kg/1 ½ lb fillet of coalfish
3 Tb flour
1 Tb salt
½ tsp pepper
2–3 large onions
4 Tb butter or margarine for frying

Slice onions thin and brown them evenly in the butter.

But the fish fillets about 5 cm/2 inches thick. Dredge them in flour, salt and pepper, and fry them in butter about 5–10 minutes.

Arrange the fish on a warm platter garnished with fried onions. Serve with boiled potatoes and carrot salad (see page 67).

Herring Flounder

Sildeflyndrer

The name of this dish derives from the way in which it is prepared. The herrings are split open and lain flat, two together with skin sides out. The resemblance to a flounder is evident.

Ingredients

1 kg/2 lb fresh herring
2 Tb chopped parsley
2 Tb chopped dill
2 Tb chopped chives
4 Tb flour
1 Tb salt
1 tsp pepper
butter or margarine for frying

Clean herring and remove back bones without tearing the fish in two. Cut off fins. Lay half of the herring flat, skin side down. Mix the chopped herbs and spread them over the insides of the fish. Cover with another herring, skin side up, and press the «flounder» firmly together.

Dredge the «flounder» in a mixture of flour, salt and pepper, and fry them golden brown in butter.

Serve herring flounder with boiled potatoes and carrot salad (see page 67).

Young mackerel may be prepared in the same way.

Herring Pancakes
Sildepannekaker

It is best to use sprat or brisling for this dish, but, if they are not available, herring may be substituted. It is delicious either way.

Ingredients
¾ kg/1 ½ lb brisling, sprat
*   or young herring*
butter for frying
8 Tb flour
½ liter/1 pint milk
¼ tsp salt
3 eggs
2–3 Tb chopped chives

Clean the fish as follows: Cut off the tail. Cut a nick in the belly of the fish at the neck and tear off the head so the entrails follow. It is unnecessary to remove the tails of brisling or sprat. Rinse off fish scales and dry the fish. Brown butter in a frying pan. Lay the fish tightly together in the frying pan, with tails toward the middle. Fry golden brown and flip pan to brown the other side.

Make pancake batter of the flour, milk, eggs and salt and pour it over the browned fish. Fry until brown underneath and turn carefully – for example on a flat pan cover. Fry the other side until the pancake is barely set.

The amounts given should be enough for three pancakes.

Serve with a green salad and bread.

Lightly Salted Fish
Sprengt fisk

Lightly salted fish is always sold in fillets. Cod and coalfish are most common. The fish is so sparingly salted that it is unnecessary to soak it before cooking.

Ingredients
1 kg/2 lb lightly salted fish
water

Melted Butter with Chopped Eggs
(Eggesmør)
2 hard-boiled eggs
about 100 g/3 ½ oz/½ cup butter

Rinse fish fillets and cut them in approx. 5 cm/2 inch thick slices. Bring water to a boil – do not salt – and add fish. Poach for about 7 minutes.

Arrange fish on a warm platter and serve with boiled carrots, potatoes and melted butter to which the finely chopped hard-boiled eggs have been added.

Smoked Haddock à la Bergen
Røkt kolje som i Bergen

In Bergen the tail end of large cod or haddock is smoked and used in this dish. In other regions of the country, the whole haddock is usually smoked and prepared in the same way.

Ingredients
about 1 kg/2 lb smoked haddock
butter for browning
2–3 dl/1 cup/1 cup low fat sour cream

Skin the fish and cut it into large slices. Brown pieces in butter. Pour sour cream over, cover and let the fish simmer until the back bone is easily removed – about 15 minutes. Arrange on a warm platter and pour the sauce over.

Serve with potatoes and boiled carrots.

Fish Soufflé

Fiskegrateng

Fish soufflé may be made with any kind of fish. The fish may be cooked or raw, fresh, smoked, salted or even lye-soaked (see page 23).

Ingredients
approx. 500 g/1 lb raw or cooked fish,
    cleaned and boned
2 Tb butter
4 Tb flour
4 dl/1 ⅓ cups/1 ¾ cups milk
salt
1 tsp ground nutmeg
3–4 eggs
2–3 Tb dried bread crumbs

Oven temperature: 200 °C/390 °F
Baking time: ¾–1 hour

Make a thick white sauce of butter, flour and milk. Add egg yolks, one at a time. Add fish, cut into small bits. Season to taste with salt and pepper. Beat egg whites stiff and fold them into the sauce. Pour into a buttered soufflé dish, sprinkle with dried bread crumbs and bake on the bottom rack of a preheated oven until the soufflé is firm to the touch and golden brown.

Serve with carrot salad (see page 67), softened butter and bread.

Pluck Fish

Plukkfisk

Leftovers of cooked fish may be used in many ways. Pluck fish is one of the easiest and most popular.

Ingredients
approx. 5 dl/2 cups cleaned cooked fish
4–6 boiled potatoes

approx. ½ liter/1 pint milk
¼ tsp pepper
3–4 Tb chopped chives
2–3 Tb low fat sour cream

Pluck the fish into small pieces with a fork and cut the potatoes into small cubes. Mix potatoes, fish, chives and pepper and add milk until a thick porridge-like consistency is achieved. Heat thoroughly. Add the sour cream just before serving. Eat with *flatbrød*.

Ground Fish

Fiskefarse

Fiskemat, literally «fish foods» is the Norwegian term for all dishes made of ground fish, among them fish pudding, fish balls and fish cakes. Best results are achieved with haddock or pike. Both fish give a light textured, white dough.

Ingredients
1 kg/2 lb cleaned and boned
    haddock or pike
1 Tb salt
2 Tb potato flour or cornstarch
½ tsp ground nutmeg
approx. 7 dl/2 ½ cups/3 cups milk

The fish must be completely free of skin and bones. Grind it twice with salt and potato flour. Stir the ground fish well, preferably with an electric mixer, and add the milk, a little at a time. Shape a sample fish ball and simmer it in lightly salted water to be sure that it has the right consistency and is seasoned to taste.

Fish Pudding: Pour the mixture into a well-greased baking dish and bake it in the oven at 120 °C/250 °F for about 1 hour. Serve it with white sauce or melted butter, potatoes and vegetables.

Fish balls: Make small balls of the fish dough with a tablespoon. Bring fish stock or lightly salted water (2 tsp salt per liter/qt water) to a boil. Add a few fish balls at a time to the stock and poach about 10 minutes. Test for doneness. The time required depends on the size of the fish balls. Fish balls are often served in curry or shrimp sauce, with potatoes and vegetables on the side.

Fish cakes: Make large flat patties, and brown in butter in a frying pan. Serve fish cakes with browned butter, potatoes and green salad.

Herring Cakes

Sildekaker

The skin and bones are ground with the fish in the preparation of herring cakes. This gives a grayish dough and particularly nourishing, flavorful cakes.

Ingredients
1 1/2 kg/3 lb fresh herring
2 tsp salt
1/2 tsp pepper
3 Tb fine dried bread crumbs
6 Tb milk
butter for frying

Cut heads and tails off the herring and cut off the fins. Remove the entrails and rinse the fish.
  Grind the herring once. Add remaining ingredients. Shape flat patties and brown them in butter.
  Serve herring cakes with boiled potatoes, vegetables and pickled beets.

Coalfish or Mackerel Cakes

Karbonader av sei eller makrell

Both coalfish and mackerel are strongly flavored and are therefore well suited for many dishes made of ground fish. Their dark, grayish color makes them more appropriate in coarsely ground fish cakes than in the more delicate fish balls and fish pudding.

Ingredients
1 kg/2 lb cleaned coalfish or
  mackerel fillets
2 tsp salt
1 1/2 Tb potato flour or cornstarch
approx. 2 1/2 dl/4/5 cup/1 cup milk

Grind the fish once. Stir in salt and potato flour. Add milk and mix well. If you like, add about 1/4 tsp pepper.
  Shape large flat patties and fry them brown in butter.
  Serve the fish cakes with fried onions, boiled or creamed vegetables (see page 64–65) and potatoes.

Fish in Aspic

Fiskekabaret

It is usual to make this dish when one has left-over fish that one wants to serve cold. Fish in aspic is served with remoulade (see page 16) and bread, as a first course or for a late supper.

Ingredients
1/2 liter/1 pint fish stock
2 1/2 Tb powdered gelatin
1/2 liter/1 pint cleaned, cooked fish
2 1/2 dl/1 cup cleaned, cooked shrimp
1 small can asparagus
2 1/2 dl/approx. 1 cup/1 cup petit pois,
  canned or frozen

Strain the fish stock so it is clear and without sediment. Bring it to a boil and dissolve gelatin in it. Cool.
  Pour a thin layer of cooled aspic into the bottom of a ring mold and lay shrimp close together in the liquid. Chill until the aspic is set. Fill the mold with fish, shrimp, peas, and the well-drained asparagus. Pour the rest of the aspic over the fish and vegetables and refrigerate until the aspic is completely set.
  Dip mold briefly in hot water to loosen aspic from sides and turn out on a serving dish. Fill the center of the ring with remoulade.

Bacalao

Bacalao

Originally a Spanish dish, Bacalao has become extremely popular in Norway. It is made from dried fish – clipfish – one of Norway's major export articles.

Clipfish is a strongly salted, dried fish. The best clipfish is made from cod.

Before use, the fish must be soaked in water for one or two days. Change the water twice a day. ½ kg/1 lb skinned and boned clipfish makes ¾ kg/1 ½ lb fish, soaked and ready for use.

Ingredients
¾ kg/1 ½ dried cod (clipfish)
¾ kg/1 ½ lb potatoes
3–4 onions
1–2 Spanish peppers
2 ½–3 dl/1 cup/1 cup tomato puré
1 can/1 qt canned tomatoes
2 ½–3 dl/1 cup/1 cup olive oil

Soak fish and cut it into large pieces. Make sure it is completely free of skin and bones.

Peel potatoes and onions and slice them thin.

Layer the fish, potatoes and onions in a pan. Spread Spanish pepper, tomato puré, tomatoes with their juices and olive oil between the layers. Cover and simmer for 1–1 ½ hours.

Bacalao may also be made in the oven. Bake at 225 °C/435 °F for 2 ½–3 hours. Serve Bacalao with bread and red wine.

Lye Fish

Lutefisk (photo on page 35)

Even Norwegians do not agree about this dish. Some consider it a delicacy, others dislike it intensely. Lye fish is made of dried cod (stock fish) that is soaked, first in water and then in a mixture of water and lye. Either caustic soda or wood ash lye may be used. This treatment softens the fish and gives it a golden color and a characteristic flavor. Lye fish may be purchased from any Norwegian fish dealer from October until April. It is also available vacuum packed or frozen. But any serious lover of Lye fish will insist on making his own. Dried, salted fish, preferably cod, is soaked in plenty of cold water for 8 days. (Do not use an aluminum container.) Change the water twice daily and keep in a cool place.

Lye
4–5 Tb caustic soda
10 liter/10 qt water

Stir the caustic soda into the water and add the presoaked fish. A plastic bucket is the best container. Leave the fish in the lye mixture for 48 hours. Remove the fish and put it in a pail of cold water for 2–3 days. It is then ready for use.

1 kg/2 lb dried fish makes about 5 kg/10 lb lye fish.

Lye fish is uneconomical in use. It is best to allow ½–1 kg/1–2 lb per person.

Preparation: Put the fish in a pan without water. Sprinkle with 2 Tb salt per 1 kg/2 lb fish. Let the fish stand and steep until liquid forms in the bottom of the pan. Cover and place over medium heat. Bring to a boil, turn off heat and let the fish stand covered for about 10 minutes. Serve lye fish with boiled potatoes, creamed peas (see page 64) and melted butter or bacon fat.

Smoked Fish

Røkt fisk

As a tourist in Norway one will certainly be served smoked salmon or trout at every turn. Both are regarded as delicacies. They are part of nearly every hotel *smørgåsbord,* or buffet table, and are often served as a first course at dinner. Smoked trout and salmon are usually accompanied by scrambled eggs, toast and butter.

Refrigerated, freshly smoked trout and salmon will keep for 6–8 days. Smoked fish may be frozen for longer storage.

Other kinds of fish may also be smoked

23

and eaten cold. Either warm or cold smoke is used in the smoking process.

Mackerel may be either warm or cold-smoked. It is eaten for dinner with creamed potatoes (see page 61) and boiled or raw vegetables.

Warm-smoked herring, garnished with scrambled eggs, makes delicious sandwiches and is also eaten as a late evening snack with scrambled eggs and creamed spinach (see page 65).

Smoked eel is rated almost as highly as smoked salmon and is often found among the many dishes that make up the hotel smørgåsbord. Like smoked salmon it is eaten with scrambled eggs.

Cured Fish – Gravlax

Gravet fisk (photo on page 36)

This is a culinary treat that receives rave notices from most travellers in Norway. The best cured fish is made from salmon or trout, but cured mackerel and powan are also good. It is important to use a fatty fish for curing. *Gravlaks,* or cured salmon (usually written *gravlax* abroad), is more and more often found on menus in finer restaurants in New York and other food-proud cities.

Fish to be cured should be deep frozen a day before it is treated. This is to kill any bacteria which, as the fish is eaten raw, might contaminate it. Thaw before curing. If it is impractical to freeze the fish before curing it may also be frozen afterwards, sliced or whole.

Clean and fillet the fish, but do not flay it. Remove as many of the small bones as possible.

Ingredients
For each 1 kg/2 lb fish fillet allow:
2 Tb salt
1 Tb sugar
1 tsp coarsely ground pepper
1 bunch of dill

Mix salt, sugar and pepper. Finely chop dill.

Sprinkle a little of the salt mixture in the bottom of a platter (do not use aluminum). Spread a layer of dill on the salt and lay a fish fillet, skin side down, on the dill. Spread salt mixture and dill over the fillet and lay the other fillet, salted on both sides, head to tail and skin side up, on top. Spread dill on the second fillet. Lay a platter or clean board on the fish and put a weight on top. Let the fish stand a couple of hours at room temperature until a brine is formed. Refrigerate for 3–4 days, turning the fish twice daily.

Serve gravlax sliced very thin, on the bias. It may be eaten with creamed potatoes (see page 61) or with bread, butter and mustard sauce.

Mustard sauce for cured fish
2 Tb prepared mustard
1 Tb vinegar
1 Tb sugar
1/2 tsp pepper
1 dl/1/2 cup oil
chopped dill

Mix mustard, vinegar and sugar and add oil gradually, stirring well between each addition. Add dill before serving.

Fermented Fish

Raket fisk

Here is one example of a traditional method of food preservation that has produced a culinary delicacy.

Many fresh water fish, among them trout, char, powan and grayling may be fermented. Finest of all is fermented trout. It is fermented trout or *rakørret* that is found in fish stores in the fall. *Rakørret* is at its best around Christmas and is often found at Christmas parties, particularly in eastern Norway.

Rakørret may be frozen, but this is rarely necessary, as it is customarily served only during the cold months of the year when it may be stored cold, soaking in its brine.

It is not difficult to make *rakørret,* but

one must pay the closest attention to cleanliness during its preparation. The fish, the hands, the knives and other implements or containers must have no traces of earth on them. Otherwise soil bacteria may contaminate the fish, resulting in serious food poisoning or botulism. It is also important that the fish stand in its brine in a cool place where the temperature does not rise above +5 °C/40 °F.

Remove entrails from the fish and rinse them well. Use 3–3 ½ Tb of salt for every 1 kg/2 lb of fish. Rub the inside of the fish well with salt. Put them tightly together in a wooden tub or plastic pail, with bellies up. Sprinkle a little salt over each layer.

Press the fish under a weight and put it in a cold place. After a couple of days check to be sure that enough brine has formed to completely cover the fish. If not, add enough cold brine to cover. The brine is made of 4–5 Tb salt for every 2 ½ dl/1 cup of water. The fish is ready to eat after 3 months in the brine. Then it has a characteristic soft consistency and pungent flavor.

Serve *rakørret* with boiled potatoes, *flatbrød* or *lefse* (see page 94) and butter.

Cod Tongues

Torsketunger

Cod tongues are taken from the large *skrei* or spawning cod caught on the rich fishing banks off the Lofoten Islands. The children of Lofoten make easy pocket money, cutting and selling tongues from the discarded fish heads.

Cod tongues may be poached and served like the fish (see page 13), but they are even better deep-fried.

Ingredients
¾ kg/1 ½ lb cod tongues
1 Tb salt
oil for deep frying

Fritter batter
2 dl/¾ cup/1 scant cup flour
½ tsp salt

1 ¼ dl/a scant ½ cup/½ cup milk
1 Tb melted butter
1 egg

Rinse the cod tongues, dry them and rub with salt. Let them steep for about 15 minutes. Wipe.

Beat together all ingredients for fritter batter. Heat the oil to about 180 °C/335 °F.

Dip the cod tongues into the batter one by one. Fry them in the hot oil approx. 5 minutes, until they are pale golden brown and cooked through. Serve with remoulade (see page 16), carrot salad (see page 67) and boiled potatoes.

Boiled Cod Roe

Kokt torskerogn

The finest roe is that of the Lofoten cod, caught in the winter when it comes to the Norwegian coast to spawn. The cod is then larger than that caught earlier in the year.

Ingredients
1 kg/2 lb cod roe
1 liter/1 qt water
1 Tb salt

Wrap the roe in cheese cloth if the membrane enclosing the roe is broken. Place it in boiling salted water, and let it steep for 20–40 minutes, according to size. The roe is done when it has changed color all the way through.

Cut the cooked roe in slices and serve it with white sauce flavored with lots of chopped parsley. Garnish with lemon wedges and accompany with boiled potatoes.

Fried Cod Roe in Sour Cream Sauce

Stekt torskerogn i rømmesaus

In the cod season, which lasts from early February to early April, both raw and boiled cod roe are sold.

For this dish, the roe must be boiled.

Ingredients

¾ kg/1 ½ lb cooked cod roe
3 Tb butter
approx. 3 dl/1 cup/1 cup fish stock
2 Tb flour
approx. 2 dl/¾ cup/¾ cup
*   low fat sour cream*

Brown the cod roe whole in butter. Add fish stock and cook over low heat for about 15 minutes.

Thicken stock slightly with flour, blended with a little cold water. Season to taste with salt and pepper.

Cut the roe in slices and serve it with the sauce, brussels sprouts, potatoes and stirred lingonberries (see page 72) or cranberry sauce.

Cod Roe Caviar

Torskerognkaviar

Caviar made of cod roe is much in demand as a sandwich spread. During the winter, when the cod's roe is large, one can make caviar at home.

Ingredients

1 kg/2 lb cod roe
1 Tb salt
2 tsp sugar
1 dl oil

Rub the roe with the salt and sugar mixture, without breaking the outer membrane. Let it stand and steep, refrigerated, for about 36 hours.

Have the roe cold-smoked, or prepare it without smoke.

Scrape the roe from the membrane and mix it thoroughly with the oil. Season, if desired, with more salt.

Spoon the caviar into small jars and pour a little oil on top. Caviar will keep 2–3 weeks refrigerated. Freeze for longer storage.

Caviar of Salmon or Trout Roe

Kaviar av laks eller ørretrogn

The coarse roe of salmon and trout makes an especially fine caviar that is used as a first course, often combined with cured salmon or trout.

Ingredients

250 g/½ lb salmon or trout roe
2 tsp salt
½ tsp sugar
1 Tb oil
2 tsp cognac

Rub the roe with salt and sugar, without breaking the outer membrane, and let it stand refrigerated for 48 hours.

Dip the roe in boiling water for 20 seconds. Scrape the roe from the membrane and drain well.

Add oil and cognac, stir well and season to taste with salt. Refrigerate the roe for 2–3 days before serving.

The roe will keep for about 1 week, refrigerated. Freeze for longer storage.

Capelin Caviar

Lodderognkaviar (photo on page 36)

This fine-grained, golden-yellow caviar is made from the roe of the capelin. A small fish, belonging to the smelt family, capelin is caught in great quantities in waters off the northern coast of Norway and in the Barents Sea. The fish itself is not eaten in Norway, but caviar made from its roe is regarded as gourmet fare.

Capelin caviar is served mainly as a appetizer with finely chopped onions or chives and sour cream. It may also be used as a garnish for dishes of, for example, salmon, trout or sole. Capelin caviar is available frozen or semi-preserved in jars.

In addition to the roe of capelin, caviar may be made from the roe of lumpfish (both black and red caviar), salmon and powan. These caviar varieties are used in the same way as Capelin caviar.

Fried Salted Herring with Lingonberry Cream

Stekt saltsild med tyttebærkrem

Several methods are used in the production of salted herring. The fish may be heavily salted without the use of additional seasonings. Then it is called *spekesild* – or simply «cured» herring. It may be steeped in a weaker salt solution with sugar added *(sukkersaltet sild)*, or in a mixture of salt and spices *(kryddersild)*. Yet a fourth variety is Matjes – originally a Dutch method. All of these forms of salted herring must be soaked in water before use.

In Norway, salted herring is often eaten at dinner as a main course, with warm boiled or baked potatoes, raw onions, pickled beets, cucumber pickle, *flatbrød* and butter. The tourist will undoubtedly see salted herring made into such delicacies as pickled herring *(sursild)*, tomato herring *(tomatsild)*, herring salad *(sildesalat)* and many others. On the large hotel smørgås-bord, or buffet table, one is apt to find 10–15 dishes made from salted herring. A bit of good advice: Try dark bread or rye crisp with salted herring. It brings out the flavor of the herring far better than white.

Ingredients
8 thoroughly soaked salted herring fillets
1 egg
1 Tb water
finely ground dried bread crumbs
butter for frying

Lingonberry Cream
2 dl/³/₄ cup/1 scant cup heavy cream
6 Tb raw stirred lingonberries
  (see page 72)

Beat egg and water together. Dry herring fillets and dip them in egg, then in bread crumbs. Fry them golden brown and crisp in butter.

Beat the cream stiff and add the stirred lingonberries. If lingonberries are not available, cranberry sauce makes a good substitute.

Serve the fillets warm with the lingon-berry cream and potatoes.

Pickled Herring

Sursild

This is probably the most common way of preparing salted herring. In many homes it is even eaten at breakfast, and it makes a tangy appetizer.

Ingredients
6 well-soaked salted herring fillets
6 Tb vinegar
8 Tb sugar
10 Tb water
1 onion
6–8 whole peppercorns

Bring the vinegar, water and sugar to a boil, dissolving sugar. Cool. Cut the fillets in approx. 2 cm/1 inch pieces. Thinly slice onion.

Layer herring and onion rings, with the peppercorns, in a glass jar. Pour over the cold vinegar solution. Cover.

The herring should steep in a cool place for at least 24 hours before eating.

Tomato Herring

Tomatsild

At Christmas time, as well as at other seasons, one finds tomato herring in the *smørgåsbord* display. It is one of the most popular herring delicacies, even appreciated by children, for whom salted herring is apt to be too strong.

Ingredients
6 well-soaked spiced herring fillets
  (kryddersild)
4 Tb tomato puré
3 Tb vinegar
1 Tb water
3 Tb oil
6 Tb sugar
¹/₄ tsp pepper
1 onion
2 bay leaves and dill

Cut the fillets into 2 cm/1 inch pieces.

Mix tomato puré, vinegar, water, oil, sugar and pepper. Thinly slice onion in rings.

Layer herring, onion rings and bay leaf in a crock and pour the tomato sauce over. Cover.

Let the herring steep, refrigerated, for a couple of hours before serving. Garnish with dill.

Curried Herring

Sild i karri (photo on page 37)

Even though curry is not a native spice, it is often used in the Norwegian kitchen. It is added sparingly, giving a mild flavor, unlike the strong, hot taste favored in countries where curry more naturally belongs.

Ingredients
4 well-soaked salted herring fillets
4 Tb mayonnaise
4 Tb low fat sour cream
1 tsp lemon juice
1/2 tsp mustard
1 tsp curry

Cut the fillets into wide pieces and arrange them on a platter. Mix mayonnaise and sour cream and season to taste with lemon juice, mustard and curry. Pour the sauce over the herring fillets and let them steep a couple of hours before serving.

As a variation, herring may be served with fruit, such as apples or mandarin oranges, and chopped nuts (see photo on page 37).

Eye of the Sun

Soløye

This is a tasty tid-bit that is good for a late supper with a glass of beer.

Ingredients
4 slices of dark bread
butter

4 soaked spiced herring fillets (kryddersild)
1 small onion
4 Tb chopped pickled beet
4 Tb chopped cucumber pickle
4 raw egg yolks

Butter bread and place a raw egg yolk on each slice. Curl a herring fillet around the egg and garnish with chopped onion, pickled beet and cucumber pickle.

Herring Salad

Sildesalat

There are as many different kinds of herring salad in Norway as there are cooks. Everyone has his favorite. Here is mine.

Ingredients
2 soaked, salted herring fillets
1 boiled potato
1 apple, on the sour side
2 slices pickled beet
1 pickled cucumber
4 Tb low fat sour cream
pepper, dry mustard
1 Tb brine from the beets

Cut the herring, potatoes, apple, beet and cucumber into tiny cubes. Season the sour cream to taste with pepper and mustard and color it light pink with the beet brine.

Mix all ingredients together and let the salad steep for at least an hour before serving.

Tempting Shellfish
Skalldyr

Shellfish on the table always means a party in a Norwegian home. Even in a country with as long a coast as ours, shellfish is a luxury and a special treat.

The most commonly eaten shellfish are shrimp, lobster and crab. Mussels and fresh-water crayfish are also often available. Salt-water crayfish is also to be had from time to time.

Lobster, crab, crayfish and mussels are sold raw or boiled, but shrimp and salt-water crayfish are boiled on the fishing boats as soon as they are pulled from the sea. Shrimp may be bought all year round, either fresh or frozen.

Lobster, by law, may not be caught between July 15 and September 30. No matter. It is, in any case, at its best at Christmas time.

The crab season is from the end of September until around Christmas.

The crayfish season is very short – from the beginning of August to mid-September, but Norway imports deep-frozen Turkish salt-water crayfish that may be purchased all year round.

Mussels are in season from the end of September until April.

Oysters may be bought in special fish stores for a brief period, beginning just before Christmas and ending in mid-winter. Oysters, however, are rarely eaten in Norway.

It may surprise foreigners to learn that Norwegians generally eat their shellfish plainly boiled and cold, with simple accessories like mayonnaise, lemon, bread and butter.

Lobster and crab are roughly cleaned. The stomach and intestines are removed from lobster, the gills are removed from crab. The claws are cracked and the meat is served in the shell. Shrimp (photo on page 38) and crayfish are served in their shells. The charm and fun of eating shellfish lies in the fact that one cleans them oneself at the table.

Mussels, shrimp and crab are sometimes prepared with sauces and in stews, in addition to being eaten boiled.

Creamed Shellfish
Skalldyrstuing

Crab, shrimp and mussels are often eaten creamed. To stretch the dish one may add small cubes of fish pudding to the sauce.

Creamed shellfish is spooned into pastry shells or tarts and served at late suppers or as a first course at dinner.

Ingredients
2 crabs or
½ kg/1 lb cleaned shrimp or
28–30 mussels

3 Tb butter
3 Tb flour
4 dl/1 ⅓ cup/1 ½ cup light cream
salt
cayenne pepper
2 Tb sherry

Clean the shellfish and coarsely chop them.

Make a sauce with the butter, flour and cream. Season to taste with salt, cayenne pepper and sherry. Add shellfish. Just before serving stir in 1 Tb of butter to give the sauce a sheen.

Crayfish Tails in Dill Sauce

Krepsehaler i dillsaus

This dish is best made with the tails of fresh-water crayfish, but salt-water crayfish tails are a satisfactory substitute.

Ingredients
16–20 crayfish tails
1 bunch of dill
3 dl/1 cup/1 ¼ cup crayfish stock
juice of ½ lemon
4 dl/1 ⅓ cups/1 ½ cups cream
1 Tb butter
1 ½ Tb flour
a pinch of cayenne pepper
salt

Clean the crayfish. Cover shells with cold water, bring to a boil and skim. Simmer stock about 10 minutes. Strain and taste. If it is too salty add water.

Coarsely chop dill stems and sauté them for a couple of minutes in a little butter. Add crayfish stock and lemon juice. Cook about 15 minutes. Strain stock and boil it until reduced by half.

Add cream to the dill and crayfish stock and bring to a boil. Blend butter and flour and beat into boiling stock. Season to taste with cayenne and salt. Sauté crayfish tails lightly in butter and stir them into sauce. Add finely chopped dill leaves and serve at once with white bread.

Crab Soufflé

Krabbesufflé

Ingredients
250 g/½ lb crab meat, fresh or canned
4 Tb butter
6 Tb flour
¼ l/½ pint milk
5 eggs
½ Tb salt
½ tsp nutmeg

Make a thick sauce of butter, flour and milk. Let it boil for 3–4 min.

Stir in the crab meat and the egg yolks, one at the time. Add salt and nutmeg. Whip the egg whites stiff and stir them carefully into the crab sauce.

Fill the batter in a buttered soufflé mould and bake it on the bottom shelf in the oven at 175 °C/345 °F for approx. 40 minutes.

Serve the soufflé at once with French bread and butter.

Tartelettes with Shrimps

Tarteletter med rekestuing

Ingredients
4 tartelettes
½ l/1 pint peeled shrimps
1 small can asparagus
20 small fishballs
2 Tb butter
3 Tb flour
¼ l/½ pint asparagus brine and cream
salt
1–2 Tb sherry
1 egg yolk

Make a white sauce of butter, flour, asparagus brine and cream. Add salt to taste. Add shrimps, asparagus and fishball and heat. Lightly whip egg yolk and sherry together and stir it in the stew.

Fill tartelettes with the stew and serve as a first course for dinner.

Akkar

Akkar is a kind of squid found only in Arctic waters. It is caught off the Norwegian coast. Sold either whole or cleaned, the muscular meat is firm and white, similar in taste to shellfish.

Akkar is poached like fish for about 10 minutes and is eaten with boiled potatoes and lemon sauce or melted butter.

From southern European countries, we have learned to deep fry squid. Prepare in the same way as for fried cod tongues (see page 25).

Meat in Many Ways

Kjøtt

Meat has always played an important part in the Norwegian diet. This includes both meat from animals raised for their flesh, such as beef, veal, pork, lamb, chicken, goose and duck; game such as mouse, reindeer and deer; as well as such birds as wild duck, ptarmigan, wood grouse, black grouse and others.

In former days, fresh meat was only to be had in season. At other times it had to be eaten salted, smoked or dried.

Today, the opposite is true. Now, fresh meat is readily available all year round, while salted and cured meats, with their traditional associations, are considered culinary delicacies that provide variation in our diet. You may wonder that there are few recipes for such meats as beef in this book. While international meat dishes are popular in Norway, I have here only included recipes that are typically Norwegian. In Norwegian hotels and restaurants one is offered a more cosmopolitan selection. To find native Norwegian meat dishes it is often necessary to seek out smaller, local dining places.

Roast Lamb

Lammestek

Norwegians have learned from other countries to season lamb with garlic and herbs such as rosemary, basil and thyme. Traditionally, however, parsley is inserted into pockets in a leg of lamb. This gives the meat a mild, fresh flavor. Allow 250 g/½ lb meat per person.

Ingredients
1 leg of lamb approx 2 kg/4 ½ lb
3–4 parsley stalks
2 tsp salt and ½ tsp pepper

Oven temperature: 125 °C/260 °F
Meat thermometer temperature:
  68–70 °C/155–160 °F
Roasting time: 2–2 ½ hours

Pierce the roast on all sides with a sharp, pointed knife and insert small bunches of parsley. Rub the roast with salt and pepper and put a meat thermometer in the thickest part of the leg, making sure it does not touch the bone. Place the roast on a rack in a roasting pan with 1 cup of water in the bottom. Roast until the proper temperature on the meat thermometer is reached. Let the roast stand and rest for about 15 minutes before slicing.

While the roast rests make the gravy: Deglaze the roasting pan with 1 cup of water or stock. Strain the stock and thicken it with 2 tsp of cornstarch blended with 6–8 Tb cream. Bring to a boil, season to taste with salt and pepper, and serve with the roast, accompanied by potatoes and vegetables.

Roast Lamb, Marinated in Sour Milk

Surstek av lam

One way to preserve meat for a short while is to marinate it in sour milk. The meat acquires a special flavor that is an interesting variation for the modern palate. Allow 250 g/½ lb meat per person.

Ingredients
1 leg of lamb, approx 2 kg/4 ½ lb
3–4 liter/3–4 qt skimmed sour milk
2 tsp salt

Gravy
1 l/1 qt roast drippings
2 Tb flour
6–8 Tb low fat sour cream
salt and pepper

Oven temperature: 160 °C/320°F
Meat thermometer temperature:
* 77 °C/162 °F*
Roasting time: approx. 1 ½ hours.

Marinate the roast in the milk in a cool place for 3–4 days. Turn it often if the milk does not cover the meat completely.

Remove the meat from the milk, dry it and rub it with salt. Put it on a rack in a roasting pan with a cup of water in the bottom.

Insert a meat thermometer in the thickest part of the roast, making sure it does not touch the bone.

Roast meat until the meat thermometer shows the temperature given above. The roast should be barely well done.

Deglaze the roasting pan with stock or water. Strain the drippings and thicken with flour blended with a couple of Tb of cold water. Add sour cream and season to taste with salt and pepper.

Slice the roast and serve with the gravy, boiled potatoes and green beans.

Saddle of Lamb

Lammesadel (photo on page 55)

This is the most commonly served roast at banquets and formal dinners in Norway.

Fall, when the sheep are slaughtered, is the best time to eat lamb, but modern freezing techniques have made it possible to enjoy it at any time of the year.

Ingredients
1 saddle of lamb, approx. 2 kg/4 ½ lb
2 tsp salt
½ tsp pepper

Oven temperature: 125 °C/260 °F
Meat thermometer temperature:
* 68–70 °C/155–160 °F*
Roasting time: 1 ½–2 hours.

Make an incision in the membrane on the inside of the saddle along each rib, so that it will keep its shape during roasting.

Remove the white membrane or cut it in squares with a sharp knife.

Rub the meat with salt and pepper. Put it on a rack with the bones down. Put it in the middle of the oven with a roasting pan under it. Pour a cup of water into the pan.

Insert a meat thermometer into one of the fillets, being sure not to touch the bone.

Roast the meat until the thermometer reaches the temperature given above. This will result in juicy, rosy-colored meat.

Strain the pan drippings and deglaze the pan with stock. Mix deglazing liquid into the drippings. Season to taste with salt and pepper. This is the traditional accompaniment to saddle of lamb, but one can, of course, make other kinds of gravy or sauce. Mushroom, Madeira or Port sauce are examples.

Serve saddle of lamb as follows: Cut the fillets from the bone and slice them carefully. Position them on the bone again, so that the saddle looks whole. Accompany with potatoes, green beans and the roast drippings or sauce.

Grilled Lamb Ribs

Sprøstekt lammeribbe

Lamb ribs may be grilled outdoors in the summer or roasted in the oven at other times. They are served with bread for a pleasant late evening snack, or as part of a more varied grill meal.

Allow 250–300 g/½–¾ lb of lamb ribs for each serving. Rub the meat with salt, pepper and garlic, if desired. Roast on the grill or in a hot oven, 170 °C/335–340 °F until golden brown and crisp, about 45 minutes. It is not necessary to turn the meat when it is roasted in the oven. On a grill, however, it should be turned once or twice during cooking.

Mutton and Cabbage

Får-i-kål (photo on page 55)

Mutton and cabbage are two foods that have been known and appreciated for a long, long time. The two, combined, constitute one of the best tasting dishes in Norwegian culinary tradition – a dish rarely found, unfortunately, on restaurant menus.

Ingredients
1 kg/2 lb lamb from the leg or shoulder
1 kg/2 lb cabbage
1 Tb salt
2 tsp whole peppercorns
water

Cut the meat into serving pieces. Cut the cabbage into chunks or thick slices.

Layer meat and cabbage in a pan. Sprinkle salt and pepper between the layers. Pour water into the pan until it is about 5 cm/2 inches over the contents of the pan.

Simmer over low heat until the meat and cabbage are tender. Many prefer this dish so well cooked that the cabbage is nearly yellow.

Serve mutton and cabbage sprinkled with chopped parsley and with boiled potatoes.

Lamb Stew

Puspas

This recipe is said to originate in Bergen. Similar to Irish Stew, it does not seem improbable that it wandered across the North Sea to Western Norway.

Ingredients
¾ kg/1 ½ lb lamb from the shoulder or leg
6–8 potatoes
4 carrots
½ head of cabbage
1 Tb salt
1 tsp pepper
2 Tb flour
water

Cut the meat into serving pieces.

Peel the potatoes and carrots, but do not slice them. Cut the cabbage into large chunks.

Layer the meat, potatoes, carrots and cabbage in a pan, seasoning with salt and pepper between layers.

Add water until it is 5 cm/2 inches over the contents of the pan.

Simmer covered until everything is done and the potatoes start to crumble.

Serve with *flatbrød*.

Singe Snout

Brennsnute

There are actually several dishes that bear this strange name. Its origin is hard to define. Simply prepared, it is a warm and nourishing meal on a cold, wintry day.

Ingredients
¾ kg/1 ½ lb lightly salted lamb
¾ kg/1 ½ lb potatoes
1 tsp pepper
parsley

Cut meat and potatoes into large cubes and place them in layers, peppered, in a pan. Add water so it reaches half way up the contents.

Bring to a boil and simmer, covered, until all is done. The potatoes should have begun to crumble.

Sprinkle with lots of chopped parsley and serve with *flatbrød*.

Lamb in Dill Sauce

Lam i dillsaus

Lamb, sour cream and dill – three good Norwegian ingredients – are combined here to make a delicious dish.

Ingredients
1 ¼ kg/3 lb lamb, cut from the shoulder
salt
pepper
butter for frying

2 ½ dl/1 cup/1 cup water
2 ½ dl/1 cup/1 cup sour cream
1 bunch of dill

Cut the meat in bite-sized pieces and brown it in the butter. Season with salt and pepper and add water. Simmer meat, covered, until it is done, approx. 40 minutes.

Stir in sour cream and lots of chopped dill.

If the sauce is too thin, it may be thickened with cornstarch.

Serve with boiled potatoes and vegetables.

Lamb Fricassee

Lammefrikassé

In the fall, when the lamb is freshly slaughtered and there are plenty of crisp, fresh vegetables, it is time to make fricassee.

Ingredients
1 ½ kg/3 lb lamb from the shoulder
2 leeks
4 carrots
1 parsley root or parsnip
1 small celeriac or 3–4 celery stalks
1 cauliflower

Sauce
6 dl/3 cups meat stock
4 Tb flour
2–3 Tb cream
parsley

Cut the meat into serving pieces.

Put the meat in a pan and add boiling water to barely cover. Add 1 tsp salt for every cup of water. Bring to a boil and skim well. Tie the green leaves of the leek, celery and parsley root together and add them to the pot. Lower heat and let simmer, covered, until the meat is tender. Remove greens when the meat is almost done and add the vegetables, whole. Simmer until everything is done.

Blend flour with a little cold water and stir into the strained stock. Boil about 5 minutes, add cream and season, if necessary, with more salt.

Arrange meat on a warm platter. Divide cauliflower into florets and cut up the other vegetables. Arrange on platter with meat. Pour a little of the sauce over the meat and vegetables and sprinkle with chopped parsley. Serve with boiled potatoes and the remaining sauce.

Salted Lamb Ribs

Pinnekjøtt (photo on page 56)

Literally «twig meat» from the birch or juniper twigs on which it is boiled, *pinnekjøtt* originated in northern Vestlandet, then wandered south to Bergen where it has become a popular Christmas dish.

Ingredients
1 rack of lamb
2 kg/4 ½ lb salt

Rub the rack of lamb well with salt. Put a layer of salt in a plastic tub, lay the whole rack of lamb on top and cover with salt. Place cold, 8–10 °C/46–50 °F, for three days.

Page 35
Traditional accessories to lye fish (recipe on page 23) are boiled potatoes and creamed peas (recipe on page 64). Browned bacon fat, melted butter with chopped egg, or mustard sauce are poured over the fish.

Page 36
Top: Cured salmon or trout is a delicacy that is easy to prepare at home (recipe on page 24). Creamed potatoes (recipe on page 61) make a good accompaniment.

Bottom: Capelin caviar (see page 26) is an elegant first course served on toast with smoked salmon and shrimp.

Remove the meat and rinse it quickly in cold water. Dry it. Hang it in a cool, well-ventilated place for 6–8 weeks. Well-dried meat may be stored in this way for several months, but it may also be frozen. Lamb ribs are available ready salted and dried throughout Norway.

Cooking: Cut up the rack along the ribs. Soak for 1–2 days in plenty of cold water, until the meat has swelled thoroughly. Place the meat in a large pan on a rack, or, as tradition dictates, a lattice of birch or juniper twigs. Add water to the level of the meat. Steam, covered, over low heat until it loosens from the bone, approx. 2 hours. Serve piping hot with boiled potatoes and mashed rutabaga (see page 65).

Smoked Leg of Mutton
Røkt fårelår

Here is another Vestland specialty that has become popular throughout Norway. This dish is traditionally served at Christmas time.

Ingredients
1 leg of lamb or mutton approx.
  3 kg/6 ½ lb

Brine
3 liter/3 qt water
½ liter/1 pint salt
4 Tb sugar

Page 37
Salted herring is found on the buffet table in many variations. Here is spiced herring in curry sauce with fruit and nuts (recipe on page 28).

Page 38
Fresh shrimp are usually served simply boiled and shelled at the table (see page 29).

Mix ingredients for brine and stir until salt is dissolved, or bring to a boil and cool well.

Put the leg of mutton in a large plastic container and pour brine over to completely cover meat. Let stand cool for 24 hours.

Remove from brine and have your butcher cold-smoke for 12 hours. The meat may also be cooked without smoking, as it is served in the Stavanger area.

Wrap the salted and smoked leg of mutton in aluminum foil and roast it in the oven at 125 °C/260 °F for 2–2½ hours or until the meat thermometer registers 77 °C/ 170 °F.

Serve cold, preferably in the Vestland manner, with *vørterbrød* (malt bread, see page 85).

Lamb Roll
Lammerull (photo on page 56)

Salted rolled lamb, veal or beef are sandwich meats that are much used, particularly at Christmas, but also all year round.

Ingredients
1 boned rack of lamb and extra
  trimmed lamb meat,
  approx. 1 kg/2 lb in all
1 tsp pepper
1 tsp ginger
1 ½ Tb salt
1 tsp sugar
1 tsp powdered gelatin
1 Tb finely chopped onion or leek

The thin layer of meat from a rack of lamb should be carefully boned so the skin is not perforated. Trim it to an even rectangle. Cut the remaining meat into thin strips.

Lay the meat strips evenly on the rectangle. Sprinkle seasonings and the chopped onion or leek between the layers of meat strips.

Roll the meat and sew it together or lash with cotton string.

Put the roll in a plastic bag in the refrigerator over night, so that the flavors blend well before cooking.

Put the roll in a pan and cover with boiling water. Add 1 tsp salt for every 1 liter 1 qt water.

Simmer, covered, for 1 ½ hours or until it is tender.

Weight the warm roll until it is cold. Slice thin and eat on bread.

The roll may be cut into smaller pieces for freezing. It will keep in the refrigerator for a week.

Roast Leg of Pork

Skinkestek

In Norway the rind is not removed from a roast of pork. The mark of a perfect roast is crackling, golden rind. The deliciously crisp rind is served with the meat. Allow 250 g/½ lb meat per person.

Ingredients
1 leg of pork with rind, approx.
  2 kg/4 ½ lb
1 Tb salt
1 tsp pepper
1 tsp ground ginger

Gravy
1 liter/1 qt roast drippings
4 Tb flour
6–8 Tb red wine
2–3 tsp mustard

Oven temperature: 170 °C/335–340 °F
Meat thermometer temperature:
  77 °C/162 °F
Roasting time: approx. 2 ½ hours

Cut through the rind with a sharp, pointed knife, making a latticework of 2 cm/1 inch squares.

Pour ½ liter/1 pint water into a roasting pan and put roast in with the rind down. Place roast in preheated oven and cook for 20–30 minutes.

Remove roast, rub it with salt and seasonings and put it on a rack in the roasting pan with the rind up. Put a meat thermometer in the thickest part of the roast. Be sure that it does not touch bone.

Return roast to oven and cook until the meat thermometer registers the temperature given above. Let roast rest for about 15 minutes before serving. Cut in thin slices and break the rind into small pieces.

Make gravy while the roast rests. Deglaze pan with water or stock and strain. Blend flour in wine and add to drippings. Boil gravy for at least 5 minutes and season to taste with mustard and salt.

Serve the roast with gravy, boiled potatoes and sauerkraut (see page 65).

Stuffed Pork Tenderloin

Fylt svinefilet

When the family is gathered for Sunday dinner, it is a special treat to find stuffed pork tenderloin on the menu.

Ingredients
1 ½ kg/3 lb loin roast of pork
12–14 pitted prunes, soaked
2 apples
butter for browning
1 ½ tsp salt
½ tsp pepper
5 dl/1 pint water or stock

Cut the tenderloin, whole, from the bone. Boil stock from the bone. Bore a hole lengthwise through the tenderloin with the handle of a wooden spoon or a similar tool.

Fill the hole alternately with prunes and apple wedges.

Lash the tenderloin with cotton string so it has an even shape.

Brown the meat in butter, on all sides, and season with salt and pepper.

Add stock to pan and simmer, covered, until the meat is done, approx. 1 hour.

Serve the meat sliced, with gravy, as for roast pork. Eat with potatoes, boiled prunes and apples, and rowan or currant jelly.

Norwegian Stew

Salt lapskaus

Lapskaus is a popular everyday dish, but it is also often served at gatherings where lots of young people are present.

Ingredients
500 g/1 lb lightly salted pork
2–3 carrots
1 slice of celeriac or 2 stalks of celery
1 slice of yellow turnip
8–10 potatoes
1 leek
3/4 liter/3/4 qt water
salt
pepper
parsley

Wash and peel vegetables and cut them in small even cubes. Cube meat.

Add water to meat and simmer about 30 minutes. Add vegetables and boil all until tender. Add leek toward the end of the cooking time. Season with salt and pepper and sprinkle with chopped parsley before serving. Eat with *flatbrød* and stirred lingonberries or cranberry sauce.

Salt Pork Pancakes

Fleskepannekaker

The combination of eggs and bacon or salt pork is well known many places in the world. This is a related dish. It is more filling and therefore often served for dinner with bread and a salad.

Ingredients
8 slices of salt pork, not too salty
6 Tb flour
1/4 tsp salt
5 dl/1 pint milk
5 eggs
2 Tb finely chopped chives

Blend flour, salt, milk and eggs to pancake batter. Let batter stand and swell for about 15 minutes. Add chives. Fry salt pork crisp and golden brown.

Put 1/3 of the salt pork in the bottom of a frying pan. Pour in 1/3 of the pancake batter and fry over moderate heat until brown. Turn and fry other side. Repeat with the remaining batter and salt pork. The above amounts should make three thick pancakes.

Place the pancakes on top of each other and slice them as you would a layer cake to serve.

Pork Ribs and Pork Patties

Ribbe og medisterkaker (photo on page 57)

This is the traditional Christmas Eve dinner in many parts of Norway. It is usually made in such quantities that left-overs make a part of buffet meals served throughout the Christmas season.

The rind on the ribs is treated in the same way as the rind on roast leg of pork (see page 40).

Ingredients for ribs
2 kg/4 1/2 lb spareribs
2 tsp salt
1 tsp pepper
5 dl/1/2 qt water

Oven temperature: 180 °C/355 °F
Roasting time: approx. 2 hours

Cut through the rind of the ribs, forming 2 cm/1 inch cubes and rub with salt and pepper. Let the meat steep refrigerated for 2–3 days, so the flavors blend.

Roast the ribs in the same way as roast leg of pork (see page 40).

Ingredients for patties
750 g/1 1/2 lb trimmed lean pork
250 g/1/2 lb fat back
1 Tb salt
2 1/2 Tb potato flour or cornstarch
1/2 liter/1 pint milk
1 tsp pepper
1/2 tsp ground clove

Grind meat and fat back with the salt, once or twice. Stir in potato flour or cornstarch, add milk and seasonings. Shape flat, medium large patties and brown them in the butter in a frying pan. Put the finished patties in the oven with the spare ribs and bake them further about 20 minutes.

Serve the spare ribs, cut into serving portions, with the patties, boiled potatoes, pan fat and sauerkraut.

Pork and Maccaroni Casserole

Skinke- og makaronigrateng

Left-over pork makes a nourishing meal in this simple casserole.

Ingredients
100 g/3 ½ oz/1 cup maccaroni
2–3 dl/1 cup/1 cup cubed pork
2 Tb butter
4 Tb flour
½ liter/1 pint milk
3 eggs
salt
pepper
ground nutmeg

Oven temperature: 180 °C/335 °F
Baking time: approx. 40 minutes

Boil the maccaroni according to the instructions on the box. Drain. Make a white sauce and add eggs, ham and maccaroni. Season to taste with salt, pepper and nutmeg.

Pour mixture into a buttered casserole, sprinkle with dried bread crumbs and bake in the middle of the oven until it is set and nicely browned.

Serve with melted or softened butter and a salad.

Christmas Ham

Juleskinke

The large, lightly salted, boiled Christmas ham belongs, by tradition, to the well-stocked Christmas buffet table. In some homes it is eaten warm with potatoes and sauerkraut at dinner, Christmas Eve, leftovers serving as snacks throughout the season.

The ham may be bought ready-salted or one may salt it oneself, as follows:

Ingredients
1 leg of pork, 4–6 kg/8–12 lb

Marinade
1 ½ liter/1 ½ qt light beer
1 ½ liter/1 ½ qt dark beer
3 liter/3 qt water
750 g/1 ½ lb salt
250 g/½ lb sugar
4 Tb dark corn sirup or treacle
2 Tb crushed juniper berries

Oven temperature: 125 °C/260 °F
Meat thermometer temperature:
*   77 °C/162 °F*
Roasting time: about 70 minutes
*   per kg/2 lb*

Bring all marinating ingredients to a boil. Skim and cool.

Rub the leg of pork with a mixture of 3 Tb salt and 2 Tb sugar and let it steep for 24 hours. Place it in the brine in a large container, not aluminum. Turn it often if it is not completely covered by the brine. Let it stand in a cool place for 2 ½–3 weeks.

The ham may be smoked after salting, but it is just as often cooked without smoking.

Put the ham in a roasting pan with the rind up. Cover it completely with aluminum foil. Insert a meat thermometer through the foil, into the thickest part of the meat. Cook until the required temperature on the thermometer is reached.

Cut the rind off the ham while it is warm. Notch latticed squares in the fat and insert cloves in the squares.

Head Cheese

Sylte (photo on page 56)

Head cheese is an essential part of the well-appointed Christmas buffet. The best head cheese is made from a pig's head, but a simpler version may be made from flank of pork. Head cheese may be frozen and is eaten as a sandwich meat.

Ingredients
½ pig's head
1 tsp pepper
1 tsp ground clove
1 tsp allspice
1 tsp ground ginger
1 Tb salt
2 tsp powdered gelatin

Scrub the pig's head well and soak it in cold water for 1–2 days. Put the head in a large kettle, bone side down. Cover with boiling water. Add 1 tsp salt for every 1 liter/1 qt water.

Cook the head until the meat loosens from the bone, approx. 2 hours.

Cut the rind off the head and pick out all meat and fat. Cut the meat and fat in strips. Remove veins and lymph nodes. Wring a piece of cheesecloth or a kitchen towel out in water and lay it in a mold. Place the rind from the head, fat side up, on the bottom and sides of the mold. Fill mold with layered meat and fat, seasoned with the mixed spices.

Cover with rind, fat side down, and pull the cloth tightly over the head cheese. Tie a string around the cloth ends, so it is held in place around the head cheese. Put it back into the cooking liquid and let it stand, just under the boiling point until it is heated through, about 20 minutes.

Weight the warm head cheese until it is cold.

Remove the cloth and slice the head cheese thin when serving. Eat with bread and pickled beets.

It is possible to substitute ¾–1 kg/1 ½–2 lb pork flank for a pig's head in making head cheese. Rub the flank meat with the mixed spices, fold it together with the rind out, lash it with string and simmer in lightly salted water until it is tender, approx. 1–1 ½ hours. Weigh it and use in the same way as head cheese made from the head.

Head cheese can be cut into smaller pieces for freezing. It will keep in the refrigerator for a week.

Liver Paté

Leverpostei

There is probably no more popular sandwich spread in Norway than liver paté. Garnished with pickled beets or cucumbers it is found on the breakfast table as well as on well-stocked smørgåsbord buffet tables.

Ingredients
250 g pork liver
1 loin pork chop
1 medium large onion
4 anchovy fillets
4 Tb flour
2 ½ dl/1 scant cup/1 cup milk
1 ½ tsp salt
½ tsp pepper
½ tsp allspice
½ tsp thyme
1 egg

Oven temperature: 125 °C/260 °F
Baking time: approx. 1 hour

Grind liver, meat, onion and anchovy fillets together once. Stir in remaining ingredients.

Pour the mixture into a well-greased mold and bake until the paté is firm all the way through.

Cool before turning out of mold.

Liver paté may be divided into smaller portions for freezing but will be somewhat coarse and crumbly.

Cured Lamb and Ham

Fenalår og spekeskinke (photo on page 58)

When you notice a nip in the air in October, November, it is time to cure lamb and ham. Dried and salted legs of mutton and pork have been hung in Norwegian storehouses for centuries, a richly traditional part of our diet.

As with so many modern culinary treats, these foods arose from the need to preserve fresh meat which, in its natural state, spoiled quickly.

Salt-drying is a method of preservation that gives delicious results. Properly treated, the meat will keep for years when it is hung well-ventilated, dry and protected from insects.

Nowadays it is usual to buy lamb and ham ready cured from firms that specialize in their preparation. Cured meat, or *spekemat*, is a term that includes mutton, pork, venison and many kinds of sausages. Not as heavily salted or as dry as formerly, the meats are more perishable than previously and must therefore be frozen if they are to be kept for longer periods.

Cured meats are considered summer food, to be served with scrambled eggs, potato salad, sour cream, *flatbrød* and *lefse*.

Allow 100–125 g/⅕–¼ lb per person.

If one wants, it is possible to make cured ham and lamb oneself. For a successful result one must have a cool, well-ventilated place to hang the meat to dry.

Brine
10 liter/10 qt water
3.3 kg/7.3 lb salt
2 Tb sugar

Mix all together and stir until salt is entirely dissolve.

If frozen meat is used it should be thawed slowly in the refrigerator before it is put in the brine.

Put the meat in a large container. Pour the brine over and put a weight on the meat so it remains covered by the brine.

Salting time: Allow one week for each 1kg/2 lb of ham to be salted, ½ week for each 1 kg/2 lb of lamb.

The meat must be stored in a cool place, but the temperature should not sink below 0 °C/32 °F or the salting process will stop.

After salting the meat should be soaked in water so that a salt rind is not formed on the surface when it dries. Soak ham for 12 hours, lamb for 4 hours.

Hang the meat in a cheese cloth or thin cotton bag, making sure that the cloth hangs loosely and does not touch the meat. This precaution prevents insects from infecting the meat. Special bags for this purpose *(spekeskinkeposer)* may be bought most places in Norway. Hang the meat in a cool well-ventilated place.

Drying time: Ham must dry for 4–5 months, lamb 2–4 months. Remember that cured meats are always made in the winter but, when once cured, keep well throughout the summer.

Slice cured meat very thinly, to serve.

Boiled Beef with Onion Sauce

Kokt kjøtt med løksaus (photo on page 17)

Boiled meat has deep roots in our country. Long before the first ovens were build, food was boiled in an iron pot that hung over the fire on the hearth. In our day, fried and roasted meat has pretty much replaced boiled, but certain recipes have been preserved and are often prepared, even now.

Ingredients
1 ½ kg/3 lb beef with the bone,
*   chuck, shoulder or brisket*
2 tsp salt for each 1 liter/1 qt water
1 tsp whole peppercorns
1–2 bay leaves.

Sauce
3 Tb finely chopped onion
2 Tb butter
3 Tb flour
½ liter/1 pint stock
4–5 Tb low fat sour cream

Boil water with salt, pepper and bay leaves. Add meat, whole. Bring to a boil, uncovered, and skim. Cover and simmer over low heat until tender, 1 ½–2 hours. Sauté onion in butter until lightly colored. Stir in flour and add stock. Add sour cream and season to taste with salt. Serve boiled meat sliced thin with sauce, boiled potatoes, carrots and celeriac, parsley root or parsnips.

Salted Beef Brisket

Sprengt oksebryst

Fiinbeck is a popular comic strip figure in Norway. He has amused generations of young and old Norwegians. Salted beef brisket with cabbage is supposed to be his favorite dish. If that is the case, he shares this preference with many others. The dish is most often served in the spring when the tender young cabbages appear.

Ingredients
1 ½ kg/3 lb beef brisket
2 Tb salt
1 tsp sugar

Brine
2 ½ liter/2 ½ qt water
500 g/1 lb salt
5 Tb sugar

Sauce
2 Tb butter
3 Tb flour
5 dl/1 pint meat stock
4–6 Tb heavy cream
approx. 1 Tb grated horseradish
approx. 1 tsp vinegar
approx. 1 tsp sugar

Rub the meat with a mixture of salt and sugar and let it stand a couple of hours.

Bring water, salt and sugar to a boil, skim and cool thoroughly. Add meat and soak about 24 hours. Rinse meat in cold water. Put it in a pan and pour cold water over meat to barely cover. Bring to a boil and skim. Simmer meat, covered, over low heat until it is tender, 1 ½–2 hours.

Make a white sauce of butter, flour and stock. If the stock is too salty, dilute with water. Add cream, grated horseradish, vinegar and sugar. The sauce should have a tangy, sweet-sour taste.

Slice the meat thin and serve with potatoes, boiled spring cabbage and sauce.

Sunday's Roast

Søndagssteken

It is still customary in many places for the generations to gather at the Sunday dinner table. Then roast beef is often on the menu – big enough to satisfy many appetites and still leave left-overs for dinners almost all week long. Allow 250 g/½ lb meat with bone per person.

Ingredients
1 rump roast of beef, approx. 2 ½ kg/5 lb
1 Tb salt
1 tsp pepper

Gravy
1 liter/1 qt roast drippings + meat stock
2–3 dl/1 cup/1 cup red wine
3 Tb cornstarch
1–2 tsp powdered mustard
salt
pepper

Oven temperature: 160 °C/320 °F
Meat thermometer temperature:
*   62–65 °C/145–150 °F*
Roasting time: approx. 1 ½ hours

Rub the roast with salt and pepper and put it, bone side down, on a rack over the roasting pan. Put a meat thermometer in the thickest part of the meat and cook until the temperature given above is reached. At 62 °C/145 °F the meat will be very rare, at 65 °C/150 °F it will be pink.

Remove meat from oven and let it rest. Deglaze roasting pan with stock. Strain drippings and thicken with cornstarch blended with red wine. Taste gravy. It should be quite thin. Season with mustard, salt and pepper.

Serve the roast with baked potatoes, braised small onions and sautéed mushrooms.

Sour Beef

Surstek

The vinegar brine in which the beef in this recipe is marinated makes it possible to store for several days. Nowadays this method of preparation is used more to add variety to the diet than as a means of preservation.

Ingredients
1 kg/2 lb boned rolled beef rump or chuck roast

Marinade
1 liter/1 qt water
8–10 Tb vinegar
1 Tb whole peppercorns
1 bay leaf
1 sliced carrot

Mix all marinade ingredients, bring to a boil and cool. Put the meat in a crock and pour the cold brine over. Marinate meat 2–4 days, depending on how sour one wants it. It must stand in a cold place.

Remove meat from the marinade, dry it and brown it in butter.

Sprinkle with salt, put a sliced onion in the pan and add water and milk until it covers the meat halfway. Simmer the meat, covered, until it is tender, 1–1 ½ hours. Thicken stock with flour blended in a little cold water. Season to taste with salt and pepper. Add cream or sour cream, if desired.

Meat in the Dark

Kjøtt i mørke

This strange name is descriptive. The meat is browned and served in a dark sauce.

Ingredients
750 g/1 ½ lb trimmed beef from the shoulder
4 Tb flour
1 Tb salt
1 tsp pepper
3–4 large onions
3–4 carrots
butter for browning
5 dl/1 pint dark meat stock (or bouillon cube and water)
5 whole peppercorns
2 bay leaves

Cut the meat into thin slices. Dredge with a mixture of flour, salt and pepper. Brown meat on both sides. Put it in a pan. Brown the onions, cut into wedges, and carrot chunks. Add them to the pan.

Deglaze frying pan with stock or bouillon and pour liquid over meat. Add peppercorns and bay leaves and simmer meat, covered, until tender, about 1 hour.

Thicken stock with flour if it is too thin.

Serve meat and vegetables in the gravy with mashed potatoes on the side.

Norwegian Beef Stew

Bifflapskaus

Lapskaus is always popular, in any of its varieties. In this version only onions are added to the meat and potatoes. The meat should be well-hung and tender.

Ingredients
750 g/1 ½ lb shoulder meat
3–4 large onions
7–8 large potatoes
2–3 tsp salt
1 tsp pepper
approx. ½ liter/1 pint water

Cut the meat, onions and potatoes into large cubes.

Brown the meat in a frying pan and put it into a large pan. Pour water over, add salt and pepper and bring to a boil. Add onions and potatoes and simmer over low heat until everything is tender. The potatoes should crumble and thicken the sauce.

Sprinkle with chopped parsley and serve with stirred lingonberries (see page 72) or cranberry sauce and cucumber pickle. Serve *flatbrød* on the side.

Mom's Meat Patties

Mors kjøttkaker

No meat patties are as good as Mom's, say all Norwegians, even though recipes vary little from family to family. The slogan just proves what creatures of habit we are.

This is one of the most popular dishes made in the Norwegian kitchen.

Ingredients
½ kg/1 lb ground beef or hamburger
½ Tb salt
1 ¼ Tb potato flour or cornstarch
½ tsp pepper
¼ tsp ginger
¼ tsp nutmeg
approx. 4 dl/a scant qt of milk

Stir meat dough with salt until it stiffens somewhat. Add potato flour or cornstarch and seasonings. Add milk, a little at a time.

Shape flat patties and fry them brown in butter. As they are browned put them into 4 dl/1 scant pint stock or bouillon and let them steep until they are done, 10–15 minutes.

Thicken the stock with flour blended in a little cold water and season to taste with salt, pepper and finely chopped onion.

Serve patties in the sauce with creamed cabbage (see page 64), boiled potatoes, and stirred lingonberries.

Mock Hare

Forloren hare

It is not easy to see how this dish got its name, for it has little connection with a hare. But it is a popular recipe that is much in use.

Ingredients
½ kg/1 lb ground beef mixed
  as for Mom's Meat Patties
  (see this page)
4–5 slices of bacon
4–5 Tb sour cream
1–2 Tb currant jelly

Oven temperature: 180 °C/350 °F
Baking time: approx. 50 minutes

Shape the meat into a loaf and place it in a greased roasting pan. Cover with bacon slices and bake the «hare» in the oven until it is done.

Put it on a warm platter. Deglaze the roasting pan with 1 cup of water. Thicken drippings with flour and season with salt and pepper, sour cream and currant jelly.

Slice the «hare» and serve it with boiled potatoes, gravy, boiled vegetables and stirred lingonberries (see page 72) or cranberry sauce.

Cabbage Rolls

Kålruletter

This dish, considered typically Norwegian, has relatives in many parts of the world. In Norway, however, it is served with white sauce seasoned with chopped parsley.

Ingredients
16 cabbage leaves
½ kg/1 lb ground beef mixed as for
  Mom's Meat Patties (see this page)

Boil cabbage leaves in lightly salted water until tender, about 10–15 minutes. Drain well.

Put a spoonful of meat dough on each leaf. Pack the leaf around the meat and tie it with a cotton string.

Simmer the cabbage rolls in lightly salted water for approx. 20 minutes, until they are tender and cooked through.

Remove the string and serve with white sauce to which lots of chopped parsley has been added.

Stuffed Cabbage

Fylt kålhode

Here is a good old-fashioned Sunday dish that is usually eaten during the winter months. It originates in an age when the housewife had plenty of time and put a lot of work into the preparation of even the simplest dish.

Ingredients
1 medium large head of cabbage
*½ kg/1 lb ground beef, mixed as for
    Mom's Meat Patties (see page 47)*

Slice a «cover» off the top of the cabbage and hollow the head carefully with a spoon. Leave a thick wall of cabbage leaves.
    Fill the hollow with the meat mixture. Return the «cover» and fasten it to the head with toothpicks.
    Put the cabbage in a pan, add water to cover, seasoned with 1 tsp salt for every 1 liter/1 qt water.
    Simmer cabbage, covered, over low heat, for about 1 hour or until tender.
    Serve stuffed cabbage with boiled carrots, potatoes and white sauce seasoned with chopped parsley.

Veal Birds

Benløse fugler

Literally «legless birds» in Norwegian, this dish is similar to many others in different parts of the world. Still we consider it typically Norwegian.

Ingredients
½ kg/1 lb lean ground beef
½ tsp salt
¼ tsp pepper
¼ tsp ginger
¼ tsp ground clove
2–3 Tb beef marrow

Sauce
2 Tb butter
3 ½ Tb flour

5 dl/1 pint meat stock
salt
pepper

Roll the meat out in a rectangle and cut it into 10 equal pieces. Mix salt and seasonings and sprinkle them evenly over the meat. Place a piece of marrow on each meat strip (bacon may be used instead). Roll the meat around the marrow and seasonings.
    Brown meat in butter and simmer «birds» in the sauce for about 20 minutes.
    Sauce: Brown butter and flour together, add stock, season.
    Serve veal birds with potatoes and vegetables.

Beef Patties

Karbonader

Actually, *karbonader* are merely a more elegant form of hamburger. *Karbonader*, or beef patties, are made of leaner meat than hamburger dough. They are practically pure beef with nothing added to stretch it.

Ingredients
750 g/1 ½ lb ground lean beef
2 ½ tsp salt
1 tsp pepper
½ Tb potato flour or cornstarch
6 Tb cold water
butter for frying

Accessories
lots of fried onion

Knead the ground beef with the salt, pepper and potato flour or cornstarch, and add water.
    Shape 8 large, flat patties and fry them in butter in a frying pan, just barely done. Many prefer them pinkish in the center.
    Serve beef patties with plenty of fried onions, potatoes or bread, and a salad.

Roast Veal

Kalvestek

From time immemorial, roast veal has been synonymous with festivity in this country. It should always be well roasted and is usually served with cream gravy. Allow 250 g/½ lb meat with bone per person.

Ingredients
2 kg/4 ½ lb veal roast,
  from the leg
1 Tb salt
2 tsp finely crushed sage

Sauce
5 Tb butter
8 Tb flour
1 liter/1 qt veal stock
  and roast drippings
2 ½ dl/1 scant cup/1 cup
  of heavy cream
salt
pepper

Oven temperature: 150 °C/300 °F
Meat thermometer temperature:
  72–75 °C/160–165 °F
Roasting time: approx. 3 hours

Bone the roast so it will be easier to slice for serving. Boil stock from the bone.

Rub the meat with salt and sage and tie it with cotton string into a nicely shaped roast.

Put the roast on a rack over the roasting pan. Insert a meat thermometer into the thickest part of the meat and roast until the thermometer reaches the temperature given above – approx. 3 hours.

For the gravy, brown butter and flour together to the color of milk chocolate. Add the strained stock and drippings. Boil gravy at least 10 minutes. Add cream. Bring to a boil and season to taste with salt and pepper.

Serve roast veal sliced thin, with braised small onions, boiled vegetables and potatoes.

Stuffed Breast of Veal

Farsert kalvebryst

This traditional dish may be eaten warm for dinner or cold, thinly sliced, on bread.

Ingredients
1 ½ kg/3 lb unboned veal breast
300 g/10 oz ground beef
1 dinner roll or thick slice of white bread
6–7 Tb pale beer or ale
3–4 slices boiled ham
4–5 Tb chopped parsley
2 Tb chopped pickles
½ sweet red pepper
1 tsp salt
¼ tsp white pepper
1 tsp thyme
3–4 Tb butter

Oven temperature: 160 °C/320 °F
Roasting time: 1 ½ hours

Slit a pocket in the breast of veal between the bone and the meat.

Soften the roll or bread in the beer and mix with the ground beef. Add the ham, cut in julienne strips, the finely diced pickles and sweet pepper, and the parsley. Season with salt, pepper and thyme.

Fill pocket with the mixture and sew shut or fasten with skewers.

Spread butter over meat, put it on a rack over the roasting pan and roast in the middle of the oven approx. 1 ½ hours.

Deglaze roasting pan with stock and serve pan juices as it is or thickened with flour.

Serve stuffed breast of veal with boiled asparagus or cauliflower and potatoes.

Veal Chickens

Kalvekyllinger

This dish owes its strange name to the fact that the meat is filled with parsley butter in the same way that chickens are stuffed for roasting.

Ingredients

750 g/1 ½ lb trimmed veal from the leg
1 ½ tsp salt
5 Tb finely chopped parsley
5 Tb butter

Cut the meat into thin slices and pound them gently with the heel of your hand.

Sprinkle with salt. Mix parsley and butter well and place equal amounts in the center of each veal slice.

Roll the meat together, lash with cotton string or fasten with toothpicks.

Brown the roulades in butter. Pour stock or water over meat to barely cover and simmer, covered, over low heat about 40 minutes.

Thicken stock with flour blended in a little cold water. Add cream and season to taste with salt, pepper and sherry.

Serve veal chickens with raw-fried potatoes, rowan jelly and boiled vegetables or salad.

Breaded Breast of Veal

Panert kalvebryst

Ingredients

1 kg/2 lb breast of veal
water
1 tsp salt for each 1 liter/1 qt water
1 egg + 1 Tb water
4–5 finely ground dried bread crumbs
butter for browning

Crack the bones in the veal breast but do not cut through the meat.

Bring water and salt to a boil, add the meat and bring to boil again. Skim. Simmer meat, covered, over low heat until tender, about 1 hour.

Remove meat from water and dry it.

Beat egg and water together and brush over meat. Dredge meat with bread crumbs and brown it in butter in a frying pan.

Serve with browned butter, boiled potatoes and vegetables.

Veal with Dill

Kalv i dill

Dill is a frequently used herb in the Scandinavian countries. It is equally well suited to fish as to meat. The fresh flavor of dill is especially good with the bland taste of veal.

Ingredients

1 kg/2 lb veal shoulder or breast
water
1 tsp salt for each 1 liter/1 qt water
1 stem dill

Sauce

2 Tb butter
3 Tb flour
approx. ½ liter/1 pint veal stock
salt
1 Tb lemon juice
4–5 Tb finely chopped dill

Cut the meat into serving pieces.

Boil the water with the salt and add meat. Bring to a boil, uncovered, and skim well. Add dill stem and simmer covered over low heat until tender, about 1 hour.

Make a white sauce with butter, flour and stock. Season with salt and lemon juice and add chopped dill just before serving. Serve meat in the sauce with potatoes and vegetables on the side.

Veal Patties

Kalvekarbonader

These especially good meat patties should be cut into triangles to identify them as veal patties and not just ordinary hamburgers.

Ingredients

750 g/1 ½ lb ground veal
2 ½ tsp salt
½ tsp nutmeg
½ tsp ginger
½ Tb potato flour or cornstarch
6 Tb milk

Breading
1 egg + 1 Tb water
dried bread crumbs

Mix the ground veal with salt, spices, potato flour and milk.

Shape the dough into a rectangle about 1 ½ cm/⅔ inch thick and cut it into 16 triangles.

Dip the patties in the blended egg and water and then in the bread crumbs. Fry them in plenty of butter over relatively low heat so the patties will be well-done without burning.

Serve veal patties with raw-fried potatoes and a green salad with sour cream dressing (see page 67).

Stuffed Veal Loaf

Karbonaderull

This bland, ground veal loaf is stuffed with scrambled eggs. It may be served warm for dinner or cold as a sandwich meat. It is popular for picnics.

Ingredients
500 g/1 lb ground veal
4–5 Tb melted butter
1 ½ tsp salt
1 Tb potato flour or cornstarch
4–6 Tb milk
¼ tsp white pepper
¼ tsp ginger

Scrambled Eggs
2 eggs
2 Tb milk
salt

Prepare the scrambled eggs first and cool them.

Mix the ground veal with butter, salt, potato flour, milk and seasonings. Shape it into two rectangles. Place half of the scrambled eggs in a strip on each of the rectangles and fold the meat together around the eggs.

Brown the loaves in butter, add stock or water and milk until it is half way up the sides of the loaves and simmer, covered, until done, about 30 minutes.

Thicken stock with flour blended with cold water and season to taste with sour cream, salt and pepper.

Serve veal loaves thickly sliced, with the sauce, potatoes and green beans.

Parsley Stuffed Chicken

Persillespekket kylling

Modern freezing methods have made it possible to enjoy chicken all year round. Formerly a spring treat, chicken was often served at confirmations and weddings.

Ingredients
2 chickens
4 stalks of parsley with tops
2 Tb butter
2 tsp salt
½ tsp pepper
butter for browning

Defrost frozen chickens. Dry them. Put a couple of parsley stalks and a spoonful of butter inside of each chicken and truss them.

Brown chickens in butter in a pan. Lower heat as far as possible and continue to fry the chickens. Cover pan, leaving a slight opening to allow the steam to escape.

Allow about 30–40 minutes frying time. Serve the chickens divided in two or four, with raw-fried potatoes and a salad.

Hen

Høns

Inexpensive and tasty, hen is often used for everyday meals in Norway. The meat is best boiled and is usually served in a white sauce. Curry sauce is particularly popular. Fricassee of hen (made in the same way as lamb fricassee) is a flavorful dish that is often served.

In this recipe the meat is combined with two other traditional Norwegian ingredients, sour cream and dill.

Ingredients
meat from 1 pre-boiled hen
butter for browning
2 ½ dl/1 scant cup/1 cup low-fat
*   sour cream*
2 Tb finely chopped dill

Cut the meat into large pieces and brown them in butter over high heat. Lower heat and add sour cream and dill. Simmer, covered, about 10 minutes. Season to taste with salt and, if desired, a little sugar.

Serve with rice, bread or potatoes and a salad.

Ptarmigan

Ryper

There are two kinds of ptarmigan in Norway. The willow ptarmigan (also know as willow grouse or red grouse) and the mountain ptarmigan (rock grouse). The feathers of the willow ptarmigan are grayer than those of the mountain ptarmigan, but there is very little difference in the taste of the meat.

Ptarmigan is usually served in a cream gravy, though hunters often grill the breast meat over the coals as a special after-the-hunt treat.

In restaurants, one is never served more than half a ptarmigan, but if one prepares them at home it is best to allow ¾ or even a whole ptarmigan for each.

Ingredients
4 ptarmigans
4 thin slices of pork fat
2 tsp salt
½ tsp pepper
gizzard and liver
butter for browning
2 ½ dl/1 scant cup/1 cup milk
5–8 Tb sour cream
1–2 Tb currant or rowan jelly

Ptarmigans are sold already plucked and cleaned. Dry the insides and rub insides with salt and pepper. Loosen the skin over the breast bone carefully and place a slice of pork fat between the skin and the meat. Truss the birds. Brown them in butter with gizzard and liver and add milk and water. Simmer, covered, over low heat until tender, 45–60 minutes, depending on the age of the birds and how long they have been hung.

Remove ptarmigans from the pan and cut them in half, lengthwise. Rub the liver and gizzard through a sieve and add them to the stock with the sour cream. Season to taste with salt and jelly. Thicken sauce with flour if it is too thin.

Serve ptarmigans with the gravy, boiled potatoes, brussels sprouts and rowan jelly or stirred lingonberries.

Breast of Ptarmigan, Pan-broiled

Stekte rypebryst

A heavenly little mouthful to be eaten on a cold evening when one isn't really hungry.

After the breast meat is cut from the bone, the rest of the meat may be chopped fine or ground, shaped into small meatballs, fried and served with the broiled meat.

Sprinkle the breast meat lightly with salt and pepper and broil a couple of minutes on each side over charcoal or in butter in a frying pan. The meat should be pink inside. Accompany with bread.

Ptarmigan Paté

Rypepostei

Henriette Schønberg Erken is often called «All Norway's Cook». For many years she ran The School for Home Economics at Hamar and her large cookbook, first published in 1914, has been the «food Bible» of the Norweigan housewife for years. This recipe for ptarmigan paté, still a specialty in many Norwegian homes, is taken from her book.

Ingredients
3 ptarmigans
1 kg/2 lb trimmed veal
* from the shoulder*
½ kg/1 lb fresh pork flank
3 tsp salt
1 tsp pepper
2 ½ dl/1 scant cup/1 cup cream

Stock
ptarmigan bones
water
1 parsley stalk with leaves
1 celery stalk

Oven temperature: 125 °C/255 °F
Roasting time: approx. 2 hours

Cut the breast meat from the ptarmigan and slice it thin. Thinly slice half of the veal and at least half of the pork.

Remove the remaining meat from the ptarmigan carcass and finely grind it with the rest of the veal and pork. Mix with cream and season with salt and pepper. Line a mold with slices of pork and fill mold with ground meats, sliced veal and ptarmigan in alternate layers. The ground meat should be on the bottom and top. Sprinkle each layer with salt and pepper. Cover with slices of pork and bake the paté until well-done, about 2 hours.

Make a strongly flavored stock of the ptarmigan bones, parsley and celery. Strain and cool. Pour over the cold paté.

Black Grouse
Årfugl

Black grouse is a larger and meatier game bird than ptarmigan. It is a rarity in our day, but the best restaurants usually offer it on their menus during the autumn hunting season. The exquisite flavor of black grouse makes it well worth trying.

Black grouse is prepared and served in the same way as ptarmigan. As the bird is larger than a ptarmigan it requires slightly longer cooking time – close to 1 ½ hours.

Capercaillie or Wood Grouse
Tiur

The capercaillie is the largest of our game birds. Young capercaillie may be cooked and served like ptarmigan. Allow 2 hours cooking time. Capercaillie is often boiled. The stock from the pot is served as bouillon before the meat course.

A large capercaillie will serve 6–8 persons.

Ingredients
1 capercaillie
250 g /½ lb lightly salted pork
water
3–4 carrots
2 parsley roots or parsnips
1–2 leeks

Flay the capercaillie. Cut it into four pieces so it will take less room in the pot.

Put the meat in the pot with the neck and giblets and the salt pork. Pour over boiling water to barely cover. Bring to a boil and skim. Cover and simmer over low heat until tender, approx. 2 ½ hours.

Put the vegetables in the pot so they will be done at the same time as the meat.

Slice meat and pork and cut vegetables into oblong strips. Make a white sauce with some of the cooking stock and serve it with the meat, vegetables and mashed potatoes.

Roast Reindeer
Rensdyrstek (photo on front cover shows roasted saddle of reindeer)

Reindeer is the most commonly eaten game in Norway. The meat has a unique and delicious flavor. It should be lightly roasted so the delicate flavor comes into its own.

All parts of the animal may be roasted, but the haunch and saddle are generally served on special occasions. The saddle is roasted and served in the same way as saddle of lamb (see page 32).

Nowadays the haunch is often sold boned and rolled. This makes it easier to cook and makes for evener serving slices. Allow 250 g/½ lb meat per person.

Ingredients
2 kg/4 lb boned and rolled haunch of
*   reindeer*
10 coarsely crushed juniper berries
2 tsp pepper

Sauce
1 liter/1 qt roasting juices and stock
2 ½ Tb flour
6–8 Tb sour cream
5 finely crushed juniper berries
1 Tb currant or rowan jelly
2–3 slices of geitost
*   (brown goat cheese)*

Oven temperature: 125 °C/255 °F
Meat thermometer temperature:
*   70–77 °C/160–170 °F*
Roasting time: 2–3 hours

Rub the roast with juniper berries and pepper and put it on a rack over a roasting pan. Insert a meat thermometer in the middle of the roast and pour a little water into the pan. Put the pan in the middle of the oven. Cook until the meat thermometer registers the above indicated temperature. At 70 °C/ 160 °F the meat will be rosy, at 77 °C/170 °F it will be well done. Tastes vary, but the meat must never be cooked so long that it is dry.

Deglaze the roasting pan with stock. Strain the pan juices and thicken them with flour blended in a little cold water. Boil the gravy at least 10 minutes, add sour cream and season to taste with jelly and, if desired, geitost (brown goat cheese) which many believe enhances the gamey flavor. Thinly slice the meat and serve it with the gravy, boiled potatoes, brussels sprouts and stewed apple halves filled with jelly.

Finnish Beef
Finnbiff

Finnish beef is the name give to the paper-thin slices of meat cut from the shoulder, chuck or rib of reindeer (moose is also used at times). Slicing is easiest when the meat is semi-frozen. Finnish beef may also be bought ready-sliced and frozen in packages of ½ kg/1 lb.

Ingredients
500 g/1 lb Finnish beef
1 large onion
butter for frying
1 tsp salt
2 ½ dl/1 scant cup/1 cup dark beer
4–6 Tb sour cream

Slice the onion in thin rings and brown it, together with the meat. The meat need not be completely defrosted before browning.

Page 55
Top: Saddle of lamb is party food. It may be seasoned in the traditional manner with parsley (recipe on page 32) or, as here, with rosemary.

Bottom: Mutton and cabbage is a popular dish throughout Norway (recipe on page 33).

Page 56
Top: Salted lamb ribs (recipe on page 34) is a specialty from Western Norway (Vestlandet) that has become popular in other parts of the country as well. It is served with mashed rutabaga (recipe on page 65).

Bottom: Home made head cheese (recipe on page 43) and lamb roll (recipe on page 39) belong on the table at Christmas and are especially good eaten with *lefse* (recipe on page 94).

Sprinkle with salt and add beer (or water). Add sour cream and simmer, covered, over low heat until tender, approx. 20 minutes.

The cooking juices may be thickened with 2 tsp cornstarch if desired.

Serve Finnish beef with boiled brussels sprouts, mashed potatoes and stirred lingonberries (see page 72) or cranberry sauce.

Boiled Reindeer

Kokt rensdyrkjøtt

Reindeer meat has been boiled from earliest times, particularly by the nomadic Lapps who had limited cooking facilities. Herding the reindeer on the mountain plains, it was practical to prepare a whole dinner in one big pot. Boiling reindeer produces a flavorful broth that is drunk along with the delicious meat.

Page 57
Top: Sausages and pork patties (recipe on page 41) are eaten at Christmas many places in Norway.

Bottom: Pork ribs with a crisp latticed rind is often served with pork sausages and pork patties at the festive Christmas Eve dinner (recipe on page 41).

Page 58
Top: Cured lamb and ham (recipe on page 44) make delicious summer eating. On special occasions they are accompanied by beer and aquavit.

Bottom: Rich, delicious sour cream porridge (recipe on page 69) is still party food throughout most of Norway.

Ingredients
1 ½ kg/3 lb reindeer meat from
the shoulder or breast
1 tsp salt for each 1 liter/1 qt water
2 carrots
2–3 parsley stalk with tops
1 slice of rutabaga (yellow turnip)
1 tsp whole peppercorns

Crack the bones to simplify cutting the meat into serving pieces when cooked.

Bring water and salt to a boil and add meat. Bring to a boil, uncovered, and skim. Add carrots, parsley and rutabaga and simmer, covered, over low heat until the meat is tender, about 1 ½ hours. Cut meat into serving pieces and serve with boiled potatoes and creamed peas (see page 64). Serve the broth with the meat. The vegetables that were cooked with the meat may be diced and added to the broth.

Reindeer Tongues

Rensdyrtunger

This is a delicacy most commonly eaten in regions where reindeer are often hunted – particularly in the northern parts of the country. The tongues are quite small so one should allow 2 to a person.

Ingredients
8 reindeer tongues
6–8 Tb salt

Thaw tongues if frozen. Rub them with salt and let them steep for approx. 24 hours.

Rinse off the salt and place tongues in a pan. Add water to cover. Bring to a boil, uncovered, and skim. Simmer, covered, over low heat until tender, 1 ½–2 hours. Remove tongues from pan and rinse them under cold, running water. Remove the skin.

Cut tongues in half, lengthwise, and serve them with mashed rutabaga (see page 65), potatoes or *flatbrød* and with some of the cooking juices as sauce.

Fillet of Moose with Chanterelles

Elgfilet med kantareller

Moose tastes a lot like beef but is a bit sweeter. Like beef, moose is tenderized by hanging. It is prepared and served in the same way as beef. Allow 250 g/½ lb meat per person.

Ingredients

approx. 1 ½ kg/3 lb fillet or
*   tenderloin of mooose*
1 bottle of red wine
5–6 coarsley crushed juniper berries
1 bay leaf
1 tsp salt
1 onion
1 tsp whole peppercorns
1 liter/1 qt cleaned chanterelles

Oven temperature: 225 °C/440 °F
Meat thermometer temperature:
*   62–65 °C/142–150 °F*
Roasting time: approx. 30 minutes

Bone the meat and lash the fillet with cotton string so it has an even shape. Marinate it overnight in red wine to which the juniper berries and bay leaf have been added.

Dry the fillet and brown it quickly in butter. Sprinkle with salt.

Crack the bone and put it in the roasting pan with coarsely chopped onion and pepper. Pour the red wine marinade over.

Put the moose fillet over the bone and roast it at temperature indicated above for about 30 minutes.

Brown the chanterelles quickly in butter and season with salt and pepper.

Slice the fillet and serve it with the chanterelles, the strained roasting juices, fried or baked potatoes and rowan jelly.

Stag Stew

Hjortegryte

Stag meat is mostly eaten in Vestlandet (Western Norway) and Trøndelag where it is hunted. The meat is tender and fine-grained with a mild gamey flavor.

Stag is prepared and served in the same way as reindeer. Most people prefer it well-done, but it is important not to cook it so long that it becomes dry.

Stag may be bought in specialty stores throughout most of the country.

Ingredients

¾ kg/1 ½ lb trimmed stag meat cut
*   from the haunch or shoulder*
3–4 slices of bacon
butter for frying
12 small onions
1 liter/1 qt chanterelles
2 tsp salt
10–12 coarsely crushed juniper berries
2 ½ dl/1 scant cup/1 cup red wine
6–8 Tb sour cream

Cut the meat into large cubes and brown them in frying pan with cubed bacon. Put them in a pan. Brown onions and mushrooms and add them to pot. Season with salt and juniper berries and add red wine. Simmer, covered, over low heat until tender, about 30 minutes.

Add sour cream and season to taste with salt.

Serve with bread or mashed potatoes.

Potatoes – a Must on the Table

Poteter

A dinner without potatoes is no dinner at all in the eyes of many Norwegians.

Thus it has been for a long while, though when the potato first came to Norway, about 200 years ago, it was received with scepticism. People were sure that potatoes caused all kinds of deviltry. They were convinced that eating potatoes made one both dull-witted and ill. In fact, to this day, the myth holds that he who eats too many potatoes will grow fat and stupid.

It was the clergy that first realized the potato's nutritional value. From the pulpit they encouraged the farmer to grow potatoes and the people to eat them.

And the potato's reputation was redeemed. Today it is not unusual for Norwegians to eat 3 or 4 boiled potatoes for dinner.

In his internationally acclaimed novel *Tillers of the Soil,* Knut Hamsun pays the potato a tribute unmatched in Norwegian literature:

«What about the potato? Is it just a kind of coffee from a distant land that we can do without? Ah, the potato is an unrivaled fruit. It withstands drought, it withstands flood, yet it grows. It spites the weather and endures a great deal. If men treat it with just a little care it repays them fifteen-fold. See here. The potato does not have the blood of the grape, but it has the meat of the chestnut. It may be fried or boiled and may be eaten with anything. A man may be without bread, but if he has the potato he will not starve. The potato may be roasted in warm ashes and eaten for supper, it may be boiled in water and eaten for breakfast. What need has it for meat? The potato is small and frugal. A mug of milk, a salted herring is enough for it. The wealthy eat it with butter, the poor dip it in a little salt in a saucer. On Sundays Isak could wash it down with a swallow of thick soured cream made from Guldhorn's milk. The maligned and blesséd potato.»

Creamed Potatoes

Stuede poteter (photo on page 36)

Creamed potatoes are usually eaten with cured and smoked fish and with smoked meat. The potatoes may be first boiled, then mixed with a thick white sauce, but the dish is best made with raw potatoes. Season creamed potatoes with dill when they are to be eaten with fish.

Ingredients
6–7 large raw potatoes
2 1/2 dl/1 scant cup/1 cup water
1 1/2 Tb butter
2 Tb flour
3–4 Tb cream
1/2 tsp salt
1/4 tsp white pepper
2–3 Tb chopped dill

Peel potatoes and cut them into cubes the size of sugar lumps. Boil them half done in water.

Blend butter and flour and add to the potato water and potatoes. Add cream and season to taste with salt and pepper. Add dill just before serving.

Potato Salad, Cold

Potetsalat, kald

Potato salad is a popular accompaniment to cured meats. It is served with a dressing made of oil and vinegar or of sour cream.

61

Ingredients
½ kg/1 lb boiled potatoes
2 Tb chives
2 Tb parsley
the white part of 1 leek sliced in thin rings

Oil and vinegar dressing
3 Tb oil
3 Tb meat stock
1 ½ Tb vinegar
¼ tsp salt
¼ tsp sugar
¼ tsp white pepper

Sour cream dressing
6 Tb low-fat sour cream
3 Tb unflavored yoghurt
1 Tb prepared mustard
1 Tb lemon juice

Slice or cube potatoes and lay them in layers with chopped chives, parsley, leek rings and one of the two dressings.

The salad should steep at least 30 minutes before serving.

Potato Salad, Warm

Potetsalat, varm

Warm potato salad is a good alternative to mashed potatoes as an accompaniment to sausages or ham.

Ingredients
6 large boiled potatoes
1 medium-sized onion
8 Tb meat stock or water
2 Tb butter
1 ½ Tb vinegar
1 Tb sugar
¾ tsp salt
a pinch of white pepper

Slice potatoes. Slice onions into thin rings. Bring meat stock and butter to a boil, add onion rings and cook until tender. Add vinegar, sugar, salt and pepper and the warm sliced potatoes. Stir gently so the potato slices do not crumble. Sprinkle with parsley or chives before serving.

Potato Dumplings

Klubb, kumle, kompe, raspeball

What you call these potato dumplings depends on what part of the country you come from, as does their accompaniment.

Ingredients
6 large raw potatoes
2 large boiled potatoes
1 tsp salt
10–14 Tb barley flour
2–3 Tb white flour

Peel and grate or grind the potatoes. Mix with salt and flour. The amount of flour will depend on the kind and quality of the potatoes. Some potatoes contain more moisture than others. The batter should have the consistency of porridge. Shape balls the size of tennis balls. Some people prefer bits of salt pork inserted into the dumplings.

Lower the dumplings one by one into lightly salted, boiling water (1 ½ tsp salt for each 1 liter/1 qt of water). Season with a little thyme, if desired. Simmer dumplings, covered, over low heat until done, approx. 25 minutes.

Serve with melted butter, smoked or lightly salted pork and lamb, rutabaga and carrots.

Potato Pancakes

Rasperisk

This dish originates in Hedmark county where it is eaten with fried salt pork or sausages.

Ingredients
¾ kg/1 ½ lb potatoes
6 Tb barley flour
3 Tb white flour
(or just white flour)
½ tsp salt

Peel and grate potatoes. Mix with flour and salt and let batter stand and swell for

10–15 minutes. The batter should not be too stiff or the pancakes will be heavy.

Fry small thick pancakes in butter in a frying pan. In Hedmark sweet or commercially soured milk is drunk with this dish. You might try it with kefir or buttermilk.

Farmer's Omelet

Bondeomelett

In the country, where hard physical labor demands nourishing meals, this omelet is sometimes served for lunch.

Ingredients
8 large boiled potatoes
4–5 slices of bacon or salt pork
4 eggs
4 Tb milk
2 Tb finely chopped chives

Cube the bacon or salt pork and brown it in a frying pan. Remove meat and brown cubed potatoes in the fat. Add bacon.

Beat eggs, milk and chives together and pour over potatoes and bacon or salt pork in frying pan.

Let the omelet set over low heat. Serve it right from the pan with *flatbrød*.

Potato Patties

Potetfrikadeller

These patties can be served as a vegetarian dinner, or instead of boiled potatoes with smoked meat and fish.

Ingredients
6–8 large boiled potatoes
6 Tb dried bread crumbs
3–4 Tb milk
1 egg
1/2 tsp salt
1/4 tsp pepper

Soak the bread crumbs in the milk for a few minutes. Mash the potatoes and mix them with the bread, egg, salt and pepper.

Fry flat patties in butter in a frying pan.
Serve the patties with fried onions and a vegetable salad.

Stuffed Potato Patties

Fylte potetfrikadeller

These potato patties are served as an evening meal with bread and tomato sauce.

Ingredients
6 large boiled potatoes
1 egg
2 Tb flour
1/2 tsp salt
1/4 tsb pepper
250 g/1/2 lb cured ham
1 onion
1 Tb chopped parsley

Mash the potatoes and mix with egg, flour, salt and pepper. Make 16 thin, flat patties.

Chop the ham and mix with onion and parsley. Spread the filling on 8 of the patties. Cover with the rest of the patties, and press well together.

Brown the patties in butter in a frying pan. Serve them hot with tomato sauce and bread.

Vegetables for Every Meal

Grønnsaker

In today's Norway we revel in fresh vegetables at all times of the year. It has not always been like that. In our unfertile country with its harsh climate it has not been possible to grow many sorts of vegetables. The hardy cabbage and rutabaga have been cultivated longest, and for a long while almost exclusively – a narrow range of choice that afforded little opportunity for culinary variation. On the other hand, these two vegetables have given us such typically Norwegian dishes as mutton and cabbage and mashed rutabaga, which is eaten to this day with all kinds of smoked and salted meats.

With the introduction of Christianity to Norway, monks came from Southern Europe and settled in the far north. In their monastery gardens they grew many varieties of herbs and vegetables, thus helping to open Norwegian eyes to the value of unfamiliar produce. In the beginning, it is true, the new plants were used more in the service of medicine than as food, and «the mill turned slowly» – it took a long time for Norwegians to learn to appreciate the fine taste and consistency of vegetables.

Creamed Cabbage

Stuet kål

Meat-patties-and-creamed-cabbage is spoken almost as one word, so common is it to find these two dishes served together.

Carrots, turnips, snow peas, beans and cauliflower are other vegetables that may be prepared in the same way.

Creamed vegetables usually accompany dishes that are served without gravy or sauce, for example, salted herring and smoked fish.

Ingredients
½–¾ kg/1–1 ½ lb cabbage or
other vegetable
2–3 dl/1 cup/1 cup water
½ tsp salt

Sauce
1 ½ Tb butter
2 ½ Tb flour
4 dl/a scant 1¾ cups/1 ⅔ cups
vegetable stock + milk
salt
nutmeg

Cube cabbage (or other vegetable) and cook tender in lightly salted water. Drain off liquid and reserve. Make a sauce of butter, flour and cooking liquid and milk. Simmer at least 5 minutes. Season to taste with salt and nutmeg. Add cabbage (other vegetable) and heat well.

Creamed Peas

Ertestuing (photo on page 35)

Use dried peas, yellow or green, for this recipe. Soak in cold water overnight.

This dish is traditionally served with lye fish but is also good with salted or smoked meat dishes.

Ingredients
250 g/½ lb yellow or green dried peas
water
1 Tb flour
1 Tb butter
salt
approx. 1 tsp sugar

Soak peas overnight in plenty of cold water. Drain.

Barely cover peas with fresh cold water and cook until tender.

Blend butter and flour and stir into peas. Simmer 5–6 minutes. The mixture should be quite thick. Season with salt and sugar.

Creamed Spinach

Spinatstuing

If one orders smoked salmon at a Norwegian restaurant, it is apt to be accompanied by creamed spinach. Creamed spinach is also eaten with other kinds of smoked fish, with poached eggs and with cured meats.

Ingredients
*½ kg/1 lb fresh spinach or an equal
   amount of frozen
1 ½ Tb butter
2 ½ Tb flour
2 ½–3 dl/1 cup/1 cup milk
salt
nutmeg*

Clean spinach and remove coarse stalks. Cook leaves in a small amount of water. Drain well.

Grind or chop spinach.

Make a thick white sauce with butter, flour and milk, and add chopped spinach. Frozen spinach may be thawed in the sauce.

Scason with salt and nutmeg.

Sauerkraut, Norwegian Style

Surkål (photo on page 57)

Norwegian «sour cabbage» has little in common with the sauerkraut that originates in Germany and Alsace. Our cabbage is soured with vinegar. It is usually eaten with fatty meats like roast pork or pork ribs. It is claimed that caraway with which the cabbage is flavored aids in the digestion of fat.

Ingredients
*¾ kg/1 ½ lb cabbage – green or red
1–2 apples
2 tsp salt
1 tsp caraway seeds
2 ½ dl/1 scant cup/1 cup water
½–1 Tb vinegar
½–1 Tb sugar*

Finely shred cabbage with a sharp knife or, better still, with that true Norwegian tool, the cheese plane. Cut apples into wedges.

Place cabbage, apples and seasonings in layers in a pan. Pour water over. If red cabbage is used in this recipe, the vinegar should be added at the start of the cooking process to retain the bright red color.

Simmer cabbage, covered, until tender, 30–45 minutes. Add more water during cooking if necessary to keep cabbage from sticking to bottom of pan.

Season to taste with vinegar and sugar. The cabbage should have a tangy sweet-sour taste.

Mashed Rutabaga or Yellow Turnip

Kålrotstappe (photo on page 56)

This simple dish has a mild flavor that makes it particularly suitable as an accompaniment to strong foods such as smoked or salted meat.

Ingredients
*¾ kg/1 ½ lb rutabaga or yellow turnip
1 large potato
1 tsp salt
pepper
3–4 Tb milk*

Peel the rutabaga and potato. Slice rutabaga and cook with the whole potato in as little water as possible. Pour off water and steam off moisture.

Mash potato and rutabaga together, season to taste with salt and pepper and add milk until the mixture has the desired consistency. Reheat and serve piping hot.

65

Cauliflower with Shrimp Sauce

Blomkål med rekesaus

Should you be invited to an informal evening get-together in Norway – sewing club, bridge party or the like – you may well be served this dish, particularly in late summer when Norwegian cauliflower is at its best.

Ingredients
1 large cauliflower
1 ½ Tb butter
3 Tb flour
approx. ½ liter/½ qt shrimp stock
*   + cauliflower stock + cream*
salt
white pepper
½ kg/1 lb shcrimp with shells

Shell shrimp and boil stock from shells. (If shrimp are bought abroad they may be uncooked. In this case boil them before shelling and use this stock in the sauce.)

Cook cauliflower tender in as little lightly salted water as possible.

Make white sauce of butter, flour, stocks and cream. Boil at least 5 minutes and season to taste with salt and pepper. Heat shrimp in sauce just before serving. Do not let them boil or they will be tough.

Place the warm cauliflower on a platter and pour sauce over. Serve with bread and a green salad.

Fried Rutabaga (Rutabaga Steaks)

Kålrotbiff

In times of crisis it has often been necessary to find a substitute for unavailable meat. Thus these «steaks» originated during the 2nd World War as a popular dinner dish. Beets may be prepared in the same way.

Ingredients
¾ kg/1 ½ lb rutabaga or yellow turnip
1 Tb flour
1 tsp salt
½ tsp pepper
butter for browning

Peel the rutabaga and slice it. Boil barely tender in lightly salted water. Remove rutabaga from water and dry.

Dredge slices in a mixture of flour, salt and pepper and fry them golden brown on both sides.

Serve rutabaga «steaks» with fried onions, boiled potatoes and Furuly salad (see page 67).

Beet Patties

Rødbetekarbonader

Vegetarian food has, of course, no deep traditions in our country. For this the choice of vegetable is too limited. Besides which, our harsh climate demands a more nourishing diet with substantial additions of fish and meat.

However, in times when it was essential to stretch the supply of meat, even to find substitutes for it, recipes such as this one came into being.

Ingredients
3–4 large beets
3 large potatoes
1 thick slice celeriac or 2 stalks
*   of celery*
2 Tb dried bread crumbs
2 eggs
1 ½ tsp salt
¼ tsp pepper
butter for frying

Boil beets, potatoes and celery separately. Peel and mash vegetables and mix them.

Beat eggs and mix them with bread crumbs. Let them stand and swell a little before adding the vegetables. Season with salt and pepper. With a large spoon place flat patties in browned butter in a frying pan. Brown on both sides and serve with fried onions, boiled potatoes and raw grated carrots (see page 67).

Crisp and Colorful Salads

Salater

It has become more and more usual in Norway, as it has been in other countries, to serve a salad in addition to or instead of boiled vegetables at dinner. Many Norwegians now grow salad greens in their gardens. It is a relatively new custom, however, and arose only after Norwegians began spending their vacations abroad.

In salads, too, it was formerly common practice to use such traditional Norwegian vegetables as cabbage, rutabaga, carrots and kale.

Cucumber Salad

Agurksalat

Cucumber salad is eaten with all kinds of poached fish, but especially with salmon and trout.

The cucumbers are sliced paper-thin and covered with a sour dressing.

Ingredients
1 cucumber
2 tsp vinegar
1/2 tsp salt
1 tsp sugar
1/4 tsp white pepper
chopped parsley or chives

Peel the cucumber if the peel is thick.

Slice it paper-thin. A cheese plane is a handy tool for this job.

Mix vinegar, salt, sugar and pepper and pour over the cucumber. Sprinkle with parsley or chives before serving.

Raw Grated Carrots
– Carrot Salad

Rå revne gulrøtter – gulrotsalat

This is one of the most popular salads in Norway. It is served with both boiled and fried fish. It may also be used as a sandwich spread.

The salad may be made with a simple lemon juice dressing or with one of sour cream.

Ingredients
6–7 carrots
3–4 Tb raisins
1–2 Tb chopped parsley

Dressing
juice of 1/2 lemon
   or 8 Tb low-fat sour cream

Scrape, rinse and grate carrots. Add raisins and parsley and pour dressing over.

Serve at once.

Furuly Salad

Furulysalat

This salad is named for a popular resort in Vestlandet (Western Norway).

It is served at breakfast as well as dinner and is also used as a sandwich spread.

Ingredients
1 small wedge of green cabbage
1 large carrot
2 apples
6–8 pitted prunes
6–7 Tb hazel nuts
juice of 1/4 lemon
1 Tb sugar

Cut the cabbage, carrot and apple in fine strips. Cut prunes in strips and chop nuts coarsely. Mix everything together.

Mix lemon juice and sugar and pour it over the salad.

Stabekk Salad

Stabekksalat

This is a popular salad. It is named for the Stabekk School for Home Economics which has been teaching cooking and household skills to women and home economists uninterruptedly since 1909.

Ingredients
1 wedge of green cabbage
2 large carrots
1 leaf of kale
3 Tb oil
2 Tb vinegar
1/3 tsp sugar
1/4 tsp salt
pepper

Finely slice cabbage and kale. Coarsely grate carrots. Mix salad dressing and pour it over the salad just before serving.

Italian Salad

Italiensk salat

I cannot insist that this is a genuine Norwegian salad, but it certainly is popular.

Ingredients
1 small carrot
2 stalks of celery
1 apple
1 cup finely shredded green cabbage
1 pickled cucumber
1/2 cup mayonnaise
1/2 cup sour cream
1 ts mustard

Grate the carrot, chop celery, apple and cucumber. Mix all vegetables.

Stir together mayonnaise and sour cream and add mustard to taste.

Mix the salad ingredients with the dressing.

Variation: Add 1 cup boiled ham cut in fine strips. This salad makes a delicious sandwich spread.

Winter Salad

Vintersalat

This salad is often served on the cold buffet and goes well with both herring and cold meat.

Ingredients
1 small celeriac
2 small beets
2 large potatoes
1 pickled cucumber
1 Tb oil
1 Tb vinegar
1 Tb grated horseradish
salt
pepper
8 Tb heavy cream

Boil celeriac, beets and potatoes and dice them finely. Chop the cucumber and mix all. Stir in oil, vinegar and horseradish. Add salt and pepper to taste.

Whip the cream and stir it into the salad just before serving.

Celery Salad

Sellerisalat

This salad is very good with any kind of game.

Ingredients
1 medium sized celeriac
2 apples
5 slices of pickled beets
1/2 cup mayonnaise
1/2 cup sour cream

Cupe the celeriac and boil until just done.

Chop the apples and beets and mix with the cooled celeriac. Stir together mayonnaise and sour cream. Mix all ingredients and cool well before serving.

Favorite Desserts

Desserter

Fruit, berries, milk and cream are the commonest ingredients used in desserts in this country. In Norwegian homes today dessert is not always served at everyday meals. On Sundays and at parties it is a must, however, and on the buffet table in hotels and restaurants there is always a choice of desserts. Like all other food, desserts are influenced by the season. A midsummer visitor to Norway is apt to be served strawberries or raspberries for dessert nearly every day. Our berry season is so brief that we want to enjoy it to the utmost. During the rest of the year dessert may be any of a variety of warm and cold puddings, apple desserts, gelatin whips, fruit compotes and sweet soups. Then, there is the large and festive layered cake known as *bløtkake* or «soft cake» with masses of whipped cream. Plenty to choose from for those with a sweet tooth.

At the beach or on city streets on a warm summer day everyone seems to be eating ice cream. But ice cream is not only for summer. Even during the long dark winter months it is a popular dessert. The excellent quality and large variety of commercial ice creams, however, makes it a dessert that is rarely made at home.

Sour Cream Porridge

Rømmegrøt (photo on page 58)

It is said that porridge is the oldest warm dish eaten in this country. For everyday meals porridge was made with coarse milled grains and water, but for special occasions it was made from the finest flour and the richest cream.

Sour cream porridge has always belonged to the holiday table – both at Christmas time and at special family celebrations. It was also «visiting food», that is, a common gift from guest to hostess, and a traditional gift to the new mother during her lying in.

Sour cream porridge is still holiday fare, particularly on Midsummer Night and Olsok (St. Olav's day, celebrated on the 29th of July). On these occasions it is usually accompanied by cured meats. Sour cream porridge is made and served differently in different regions of the country. The following recipe is used in many parts of Norway.

Sour cream porridge is such a rich and filling dish that one does not need too much of it.

Ingredients
½ liter/1 pint thick sour cream
12 Tb flour
½ liter/1 pint milk
salt

Boil the sour cream, covered, for 2 minutes. Add half of the flour and stir carefully to bring the butter to the surface. Skim it off, reserve it and keep it warm.

Stir in the rest of the flour and add the milk. Simmer the porridge for 5–6 minutes. Season to taste with salt.

If one prefers a slightly tangy sour flavor, half of the milk added may be commercially soured or kefir.

Sour cream porridge is eaten sprinkled with sugar and cinnamon and with the reserved warm melted butter. Red juice, such as raspberry or currant is usually drunk with the porridge.

Milk Rings

Melkeringer

This dish, which may be eaten as a be-tween-meal snack or a refreshing pick-me-up on a warm summer day, has many names. It is, for example, also called *røm-mekolle* (sour cream bowl or bowl of sour cream, *rømme* being sour cream, *kolle* a bowl or mound) and *rømmebunke* (*bunke* is a pile or mound).

Ingredients
1 liter/1 qt milk
6–10 Tb sour cream

Garnish
brown sugar
sweet rusk or zweiback crumbs

Heat the milk to 25 °C/66 °F and stir in the sour cream. Pour the mixture, in equal amounts, into 6 dessert bowls. Cover with paper and let stand in a warm place until the milk thickens – approx. 24 hours.

Cool milk rings and serve them sprinkled with brown sugar and finely crushed sweet rusks.

Hung Milk (Creamed Cottage Cheese)

Opplagt melk

This is a very old dessert that is traditional throughout the country. It is best when made from milk soured and hung in a cloth so the whey drains off, however, in our day, it is a lot easier to use cottage cheese which may be bought anywhere.

Ingredients
1 ½ liters/1 ½ qt kefir milk
   or 250 g/½ lb cottage cheese
6 Tb heavy cream
currant jelly

Pour the milk into a cheese cloth bag or a paper coffee filter and let it drip overnight.

Mash the curds or the cottage cheese with a fork. Whip the cream and fold it into the curds.

Spoon into bowls and top with jelly.
Serve with sugar and cream or milk.

Marte Knipe

Milk desserts may be simple and inexpensive for everyday meals, elaborate and expensive for parties. Many varieties are made throughout the country.

This recipe is an inexpensive one that is intended to satisfy many large appetites.

Ingredients
1 liter/1 qt milk
6 Tb tapioca
3 Tb raisins
3 Tb almonds
1 Tb sugar
3–4 drops of rum flavoring

Bring milk to a boil and sprinkle tapioca in. Simmer, covered, over low heat until tapioca is done, approx. 15 minutes. Stir from time to time so the pudding does not stick to the bottom of the pan. Add raisins, chopped blanched almonds, and season to taste with sugar and rum flavoring. Cool pudding and serve it with a spoonful of jam.

Semolina Pudding with Red Sauce

Semulepudding med rød saus

Here is another everyday dessert that is particularly popular in families with children. It is inexpensive and filling, as well as very tasty with its flavorful fruit sauce.

Ingredients
1 liter/1 qt milk
6 Tb semolina or farina
1 Tb sugar
1 egg
2 Tb chopped blanched almonds

Red sauce
½ liter/1 pint currant, raspberry or other
juice and water
1 Tb potato flour or cornstarch

Bring milk to a boil and sprinkle semolina on top. Simmer, covered, over low heat until pudding thickens and semolina is done, 15–20 minutes. Stir now and then so it does not stick to the bottom of the pan.
  Stir in sugar, beaten egg and almonds. Cool.
  Raspberry, currant or cherry juice may be used for the sauce. Mix juice with water until it has the desired flavor. Blend potato flour in cold juice and bring to a boil, stirring constantly. Remove from heat as soon as it boils. If cornstarch is used, cook longer, until cornstarch flavor disappears — about 15 minutes. Sprinkle with a little sugar so a skin does not form on top. Serve pudding cold with lukewarm sauce.

Fruit Soup – Rose Hip Soup
Fruktsuppe – Nypesuppe

Fruit soups may be made from most kinds of berries and fruit and are served warm or cold, depending on the season. Small cookies or sweet rusks are often eaten with fruit soup.
  Rose hip soup is one of the most popular fruit soups. It is an excellent dessert that may also be purchased dried and packaged.

Ingredients
¾ liter/¾ qt fresh rose hips
1 liter/1 qt water
6 Tb sugar
1 ½ Tb potato flour or cornstarch
chopped almonds
cream

Boil rose hips in water until tender. Push them through a sieve. Measure the mash and water, adding more water if necessary to make 1 liter/1 qt.

Bring to a boil and season to taste with sugar. Blend potato flour in a little cold water and add to liquid. Bring quickly to a boil and remove immediately from heat. If cornstarch is used it must be cooked longer until cornstarch flavor is gone.
  Serve soup warm or cold, sprinkled with chopped almonds and with a little whipped cream.

Prune Compote
Sviskekompott

Fruit and berry compotes are common everyday desserts. During the winter when fresh fruits are scarce, prunes are often used.

Ingredients
250 g/½ lb pitted prunes
½ liter/1 pint water
4–6 Tb sugar
1 ½ Tb potato flour or cornstarch

Boil prunes in the water and sugar until tender.
  Blend potato flour in a little cold water and stir into prunes. Bring quickly to a boil and remove at once from heat. If cornstarch is used it should be simmered longer, until cornstarch flavor is gone, approx. 15 minutes.
  Cool a little and pour into serving bowl. Sprinkle with a little sugar to prevent a skin forming on top.
  Serve prune compote cold or lukewarm with ice cold milk or cream.

Constitution Dessert
Grunnlovsdessert

On May 17th the signing of the Norwegian Constitution is celebrated. Rhubarb is the only fruit that makes its appearance that early in the spring. A hardy plant that will grow under most conditions it is used in many desserts when it is young and tender.

Ingredients
½ kg/1 lb rhubarb
18–20 pitted prunes
2 ½ dl/1 scant cup/1 cup water
1 ¼ dl/scant ½ cup/½ cup sugar
2 tsp potato flour or cornstarch

Vanilla sauce
2 ½ dl/1 scant cup/1 cup milk
2–3 drops of vanilla extract
3 egg yolks
2 Tb sugar
2 tsp powdered gelatin
4–6 Tb heavy cream

First make the sauce: Stir milk, vanilla, egg yolks, sugar and gelatin together and bring to a boil, stirring. Stir it now and then until cold. Beat the cream stiff and fold it into the sauce.

Cut the rhubarb into approx. 5 cm/2 inch long pieces and cook until barely tender in water and sugar. Cook prunes after rhubarb. Pour off and reserve liquid. Thicken it with potato flour blended in a little cold water.

Put rhubarb and prunes in a serving dish and pour the thickened juice over. Cool. Pour vanilla sauce over the fruit before it is completely stiff. Sprinkle with a few chopped almonds.

Serve the dessert well chilled.

Stirred Currants with Eggedosis

Rørte rips med eggedosis

Even high up in the mountains in Southern Norway, one finds currant bushes growing in gardens. And throughout the country currants thrive in the lowlands. Currants have a strong and somewhat tart flavor that is alleviated by the *eggedosis* which is served as a sauce.

Eggedosis is similar to sabayon but is not cooked.

Ingredients
1 kg/2 lb currants
250 g/½ lb sugar

Eggedosis
3 egg yolks
3 Tb sugar

Clean currants and stir them with sugar until sugar is completely dissolved.

Beat egg yolks with sugar until light, thick and stiff. The sugar should be entirely dissolved. *Eggedosis* sinks if it is allowed to stand, so it should be made just before serving.

Serve currants in a clear glass bowl with the *eggedosis* in a pitcher on the side. Small crisp cookies are a good accompaniment.

Stirred Lingonberries

Rørte tyttebær

Lingonberries, also known as mountain cranberries or red whortleberries, grow wild throughout Norway – from sea level to high into the mountains. Both raw and boiled into jam, lingonberries are used a great deal as an accessory to meat and in some desserts. They are good with boiled rice and milk.

Lingonberries keep well and are well suited for freezing, with or without sugar.

Ingredients
1 kg/2 lb cleaned lingonberries
½ kg/1 lb sugar

Stir the berries with the sugar until light and foamy. The sugar should be completely dissolved.

Pour into jars and store in a cool, dark place, or freeze.

Graduation Dessert

Russedessert

A good everyday dessert that was particularly popular in families with many children. Today it is one of those old-fashioned desserts that are rarely found on restaurant menus.

72

Ingredients
6 dl/a scant 2 ½ cups/2 ½ cups juice and
    water
5 Tb semolina or farina

Use red juice, for example, currant, raspberry or cherry. Mix juice with water so it
is a little stronger than what one would
normally drink.

Boil juice and water and sprinkle semolina in. Boil pudding about 15 minutes.

Pour warm pudding into a bowl and
beat hard until it is porous, fluffy and pale.

Cool well and serve with cream or
vanilla sauce.

Troll Cream
Trollkrem

Light as a summer cloud. This is a dessert
to delight both big and little «trolls».

Ingredients
1 egg white
½ liter/1 pint lingonberries, cleaned
8 Tb sugar

Mix egg white, lingonberries and sugar
and beat with electric beater until sugar is
dissolved and the cream is light as foam.

Serve troll cream with vanilla sauce (see
page 72).

Blueberry Pancakes
Blåbærpannekaker

When the blueberries ripen in the woods in
July and August, children all go about with
blue lips. They are given blueberry jam on
their bread, wash it down with blueberry
juice. And for dessert they may well get
blueberry *soll* – simply blueberries with
sugar and milk – or, if they are really lucky,
blueberry pancakes.

Ingredients
½ liter/1 pint flour
½ tsp salt
½ tsp baking powder

2 Tb sugar
¾ liter/¾ qt milk
3 eggs
¼ liter/1 cup cleaned blueberries

Beat together flour, salt, baking powder,
sugar, milk and egg to a smooth batter. Let
stand and swell for about 15 minutes.

Add blueberries to batter.

Fry thick pancakes and pile them on a
platter. Sprinkle each pancake with sugar.

To serve, slice through the pile of pancakes as you would a pie.

Veiled Farm Girls
Tilslørte bondepiker

This dessert is easily made and goes as well
with fish as with meat.

Ingredients
3 dl/1 cup/1 heaping cup applesauce
2 ½ dl/1 scant cup/1 cup
    dried bread crumbs
3 Tb sugar
2 ½ dl/1 scant cup/1 cup heavy cream

Mix crumbs and sugar and brown them in
a dry frying pan.

Beat the cream.

Spoon browned crumbs and applesauce
in layers in dessert dishes. Top with
whipped cream.

Apples with Caramel Sauce
Epler i karamellsaus

Apples in many variations are a popular
dessert. This one has a rich caramel sauce.

Ingredients
4 large apples, on the sour side
½ liter/1 pint water
1 Tb lemon juice
6 Tb sugar
100 g/3 ½ oz/½ cup sugar
2 ½ dl/1 scant cup/1 cup milk

2 egg yolks
1 Tb sugar
6 Tb heavy cream

Peel apples and cut them in two. Remove core.

Bring water, with lemon juice and 6 Tb sugar, to a boil. Cook apples barely tender in the sugar syrup.

Brown 2 ½ dl/1 scant cup/1 cup sugar in a pan, cool the caramel a little and add boiling milk. Beat egg yolks with 1 Tb sugar.

Cool caramel slightly and stir it a little at a time into egg mixture. Heat until it thickens.

Beat cream stiff and stir into caramel sauce.

Arrange apples on a platter and pour sauce over.

Cloudberry Cream

Multekrem (photo on page 75)

Cloudberries are the most highly prized berries in Norway. They grow high up throughout the whole country. Somewhat capricious, they do not always flower and the berries often freeze before they ripen. They are therefore expensive on the market. As early as 1500 it was known that cloudberries had a healing effect on scurvy, without understanding why. Now we are aware of the fact that they contain large amounts of vitamin C.

Cloudberries store well. They may be picked right into their storage containers which should be tightly sealed as soon as filled. Stored in a cool, dark cellar, they keep in this way all winter. They are also well suited for freezing or may be mixed with sugar and stored in a cool place.

Ingredients
½ liter/1 pint heavy cream
250 g/½ lb cloudberries
sugar to taste

Whip cream stiff and add cloudberries. Add sugar to taste. Serve cloudberry cream

with cookies or spoon into sand tarts (see page 90).

Cloudberries may also be served, sugared, with plain cream. In that case, allow twice as many berries as indicated above.

Poor Knights (French Toast)

Arme riddere

When a loaf of white bread begins to get stale it may be used in this tasty dessert. Poor knights is often eaten instead of pancakes following pea soup.

Ingredients
4 slices of white bread
1 egg
1 Tb sugar
8 Tb milk
¼ tsp cardamom or cinnamon
butter for frying

Page 75
Top: Cloudberry cream (recipe on page 74) and rosettes (recipe on page 93) are a dessert for the most festive occasion.

Bottom: Gelatin cream mold with fresh berries (recipe on page 80) is a light and absolutely delicious summer dessert.

Page 76
Top: Home made bread always tastes good. *Above:* Kneipp bread (recipe on page 83) and Christmas stollen (recipe on page 85). *In the middle:* white bread, braided (recipe on page 83). *Below:* malt bread with raisins sprinkled with chopped nuts (recipe on page 85).

Bottom: Coffee Ring is a tradition on the birthday table (recipe on page 85).

Beat egg and sugar together and add milk and seasonings. Soak bread well in egg mixture.

Fry bread slices golden brown on both sides in butter in a frying pan.

Serve at once with jam. Topped with a spoonful of whipped cream the «knights» grow «rich» at once.

Bread Pudding

Brødpudding

Throughout our history, Norwegians have learned never to waste food – not even old stale bread. It is dried and ground, so that there are always crumbs for dredging meat and fish and for a variety of desserts.

Warm bread pudding with red sauce is a popular winter dessert.

Ingredients
100 g/3 ½ oz/12 ½ Tb dry bread crumbs
2 ½ dl/1 scant cup/1 cup milk
2 Tb sugar
4–5 Tb raisins or dried currants
grated peel and juice of ½ lemon
2 eggs

Page 77
Top: Cream layer cake (recipe on page 86) may be topped with canned fruits and grated chocolate as here. Other suggestions for fillings and toppings are given on page 87.

Bottom: Mother Monsen is a moist and tasty cake that is baked in the roasting pan or a flat cake tin (recipe on page 87).

Page 78
Macaroon wreath cake, decorated with flags and paper snappers, belongs on the table at special occasions (recipe on page 88).

Oven temperature: 175 °C/345 °F
Baking time: 30–40 minutes

Pour milk over bread and let stand and swell for a few minutes.

Add remaining ingredients and pour into a greased casserole. Bake on bottom rack of oven until the pudding is set and nicely browned.

Serve bread pudding warm with red sauce (see page 71) or jam.

Barley Omelet

Byggmelsomelett

An easy warm dessert that is good after a soup dinner.

Ingredients
5 Tb barley flour
3 dl/1 cup/a little more than 1 cup milk
2 Tb sugar
2–3 drops of almond flavoring
3 eggs

Oven temperature: 180 °C/355 °F
Baking time: 30–40 minutes

Blend flour and cold milk and bring to a boil, stirring constantly.

Season to taste with sugar and almond flavoring and add egg yolks.

Beat egg whites stiff and fold them into the batter.

Pour into a greased casserole and bake omelet in the middle of the oven until it sets.

Serve warm with red sauce (see page 71) or jam.

Princess Pudding

Prinsessepudding

Warm desserts are particularly well suited to our cold climate. This pudding is a traditional Sunday dessert, golden brown and light as air.

Ingredients
2 Tb butter
4 Tb flour
12 Tb milk
3 Tb coarsely chopped almonds
2 Tb sugar
3 eggs

Make a thick white sauce of butter, flour and milk.

Separate eggs and beat whites stiff.

Stir egg yolks into white sauce with almonds and sugar.

Fold whites carefully into batter.

Pour into a well-greased casserole, cover with aluminum foil.

Place casserole on a rack in a pan and add water until it is half way up the casserole.

Cook pudding until set, about 45 minutes.

Serve princess pudding warm with red sauce (see page 71) or jam.

Sour Milk Bavarian

Surmelksfromasj

Bavarian creams of all sorts are always a welcome dessert. On a restaurant dessert table one will always find at least one Bavarian, often several.

Bavarians can be made with sour milk and cream as in this case. They may be flavored with fruit, berries, fruit juice or wine.

Ingredients
2 ½ Tb powdered gelatin
2 ½ dl/1 scant cup/1 cup heavy cream
5 dl/1 pint kefir or cultured sour milk
3 Tb sugar
3 Tb chopped almonds
1 tsp vanilla sugar or ½ tsp vanilla extract

Soften and dissolve gelatin as indicated on package.

Whip cream stiff and add it to sour milk, sugar, almonds and vanilla. Add dissolved gelatin. Pour into a bowl and cool.

Serve sour milk Bavarian with red sauce (see page 71) or jam.

Gelatin Cream Mold with Fresh Berries

Fløterand med friske bær (photo on page 75)

Cream molds may be made with sweet cream or with cultured sour cream, if one likes the slightly tangy flavor. An other possibility is to mix the two.

Ingredients
½ liter/1 pint heavy cream
2 Tb sugar
5 tsp powdered gelatin
½ liter/1 pint strawberries or raspberries

Soften and dissolve gelatin as indicated on package. Beat cream stiff with sugar and stir in dissolved gelatin.

Pour into a ring mold. Refrigerate until set. Dip mold briefly in hot water to loosen gelatin from sides of mold and turn it out on a platter. Pour fresh berries into center of ring and serve with cookies.

Sherry Pudding

Sherrypudding

One more old-fashioned party dessert made with wine. This recipe calls for heavy cream, but if you want a less rich dessert there is nothing to prevent you from using light cream.

Ingredients
½ liter/1 pint heavy cream
100 g/3 ½ oz/½ cup sugar
2 Tb gelatin
8 Tb sherry (sweet or medium dry)

Mix sugar and gelatin and stir them into the cream. Bring to a boil, stirring constantly. Cool slightly and flavor with sherry.

Pour into a mold and refrigerate until set.

Turn pudding onto a platter and serve with red sauce (see page 71) or fresh berries.

March Snow

Marssne

The name of this dessert derives from the fact that it is just as delicate and fresh as new fallen snow in March. In the really old-fashioned manner it is served with canned cherries, and, because it is a typical Sunday dessert, it should be accompanied by rich Norwegian cookies.

Ingredients
2 ½ Tb powdered gelatin
¾ liter/¾ qt heavy cream
8 Tb sugar
grated peel and juice of 2 lemons

Soften and dissolve gelatin according to instructions on package. Beat cream stiff with sugar and add grated peel and juice. Stir in cooled gelatin and stir until the mixture begins to stiffen. This will happen quickly. Pour it into a mold or bowl and refrigerate until set.

Turn out onto a platter for serving or serve in bowl.

White Wine Gelatin

Hvitvinsgelé

This old party recipe proves that wine has been used in Norwegian cooking long before our time.

Ingredients
¾ liter/¾ qt white wine
¼ liter/1 cup water
1 lemon
125 g/4 oz/a heaping ½ cup sugar
4 Tb powdered gelatin

Peel lemon removing only outermost yellow rind. Squeeze lemon.

Mix sugar and gelatin.

Mix wine, water, yellow lemon peel, lemon juice and sugar, mixed with gelatin, and bring to a boil, stirring.

Strain, for example, through a paper coffee filter. Pour jelly into serving bowl and refrigerate until set.

Serve white wine jelly with vanilla sauce (see page 72) made without gelatin.

Aquavit Sorbet

Akevittsorbet

Distilled from potatoes, usually flavored with caraway, our national drink is not only drunk at meals. It may also be used to flavor this refreshing dessert.

Ingredients
5 dl/1 pint water
250 g/½ lb sugar
peel of 1 lemon
juice of ½ lemon
1 ½ dl/½ cup/½ cup aquavit
1–2 egg whites

Wash lemon well and peel outer yellow rind with a potato peeler. Boil peel with water and sugar about 5 minutes. Add lemon juice, cool and strain.

Flavor the sugar syrup with aquavit and freeze until it has the consistency of half-whipped egg whites. Stir now and then while it is freezing. Beat egg white(s) stiff and stir them into the sorbet. Freeze until completely frozen.

Remove sorbet from freezer about 10 minutes before it is to be eaten and beat it well.

Serve in individual glasses garnished with lemon peel or toasted almonds. Serve with *kransekake* (macaroon wreath cake, see page 88) if desired.

Home-made Bread and Cakes

Brød og kaker

When you go into a Norwegian bakery you will invariably find a large selection of breads. The selection will differ from bakery to bakery, from region to region, yet whatever choice you make, in whatever part of the country, you are bound to get good bread. Unbleached white flour and coarsely milled whole grained flours contribute to this consistent excellence.

Nor is it only bakeries that bake bread in Norway. In recent years home-baking has become more and more popular. The home-baker can decide for herself just how dark or light the bread should be and may be sure of having fresh bread in the house whenever she wants.

Bread plays a different role in Norway than in most other countries. Buttered, with different spreads, it is eaten for breakfast, lunch and before bed-time snacks. It rarely accompanies the evening meal, when it is customary instead to eat that very Norwegian product, *flatbrød*. Not too long ago *flatbrød* was always kept in a drawer in the kitchen table, making it a simple matter to help oneself to the crisp wafers at any time.

Just as typically Norwegian as *flatbrød*, *lefse* resembles a thin pancake. It is eaten buttered, spread with sugar and cheese and eaten both at everyday meals and at parties. There is a seemingly limitless number of lefse recipes, differing from region to region. Everyday *lefse* is made from inexpensive ingredients, but on special occasions butter, cream and finely milled flours are used.

The oldest cakes we know of were baked on irons over the fire on the hearth. These «small cakes» or cookies are still made for holidays and special occasions. Oven-baked cakes and cookies were not known until much later – probably not before 1800 – when masonry ovens appeared in the home.

A large variety of cakes is baked in Norway today. Cookies and cakes are usually served with after-dinner coffee – in most homes a daily must – and as an accompaniment to dessert. Cakes are also brought out whenever the urge for «something good» presents itself.

At Christmas time cakes play a special role. Traditionally at least 7 different kinds of «small cakes» or rich Christmas cookies are baked in every home. In some homes as many as 9 or even 11 varieties were made – always an uneven number as odd numbers were considered lucky. In former times the number was an indication of your wealth – a kind of status symbol. Which kinds are chosen differs from place to place and from family to family. The most commonly baked, for which recipes may be found in this book, are Berlin wreaths, stacks of planks, sand tarts, goro, strull, curled cookies, poor man and stag's antlers. In many families a dark cake, such as syrup snaps, is also baked.

Christmas cookies are served to guests with a glass of wine at midday, with coffee after dinner.

Christmas is certainly the only time of year when the children are allowed to eat as many cakes as they like.

82

Basic Bread Recipe

For home baking it is not necessary to have more than one basic bread recipe. By varying the proportions of different flours (see page 102 for information about Norwegian flour types) one may bake bread that is just as dark or as light as one wishes.

Both fresh and dry yeast may be used. There are two kinds of dry yeast – one should be blended in luke-warm liquid before use, the other mixed right into the flour. The recipes for bread and other yeasted baked goods in this book are based on fresh yeast sold in 50 g/1 ¾ oz packages. Dry yeast packages are sold in similar quantities.

Ingredients
50 g/1 ¾ oz yeast
½ liter/1 pint water
1 liter/1 qt skimmed milk, sweet or sour
1 Tb salt
2–2 ½ kg/4–5 lb flour

Oven temperature:
200–225 °C/390–435 °F
Baking time: 30–45 minutes

Mix dough in the usual way: Stir yeast into water, add milk, salt and most of the flour. Knead dough well, adding more flour as needed, until firm and smooth. Cover well and let rise in a warm place for 2–3 hours.

Knead dough again, divide into 3 og 4 equal loaves. Dark bread is usually baked in tins, white is shaped into loaves on a baking sheet. One may, however, do as one likes about this, varying the shape of the bread according to one's own imagination.

Let bread rise in loaves 20–30 minutes and bake on lowest rack in oven. Use lower temperature for dark bread, but, as always in baking, test for best temperature and baking time on your own oven.

Dark Rye Bread

Grovt rugbrød (photo on page 76)

Use 1 part dark coarsely milled whole grain rye (grov sammalt rug), 1 part finely milled whole grain rye, 1 part sifted rye (rugmel) and 1 part white flour. Add 3–4 Tb dark syrup if desired.

Kneipp Bread

Use 1 part coarsely milled whole wheat and 1 part finely milled whole wheat.

Kneipp White Bread

Use 1 part coarsely or finely milled whole wheat and 1 part white.

White Bread

Loff (photo on page 76)

Use only white flour and add 2–3 Tb oil or melted butter. The dough may be braided as shown on photo.

Long Bread

Langebrød

Use 1 part sifted rye and 1 part white.

Rolls and Crescents

Rundstykker og horn

Both rolls and crescents are often eaten at lunch and breakfast on Saturdays and Sundays. They may be successfully frozen so that one always has the freshly baked product on hand. Makes 16 rolls or crescents.

Ingredients
50 g/1 ¾ oz yeast
½ liter/1 pint milk
4 Tb melted butter
1 tsp salt
1 tsp sugar
approx. 750 g/1 ½ lb flour

Oven temperature: 225 °C/435 °F
Baking time: approx. 15 minutes

Stir yeast into luke-warm milk. Add remaining ingredients and knead dough well. For white rolls and crescents use only white flour. For darker breads use equal parts of coarsely and finely milled whole wheat and white.

Cover dough well and let rise in a warm place for 45–60 minutes. Knead briefly.

Rolls
Divide dough into 16 equal parts and shape into round rolls.

Crescents
Divide dough into two equal parts. With rolling pin roll each piece into a large circle about 30–35 cm/12–14 inches in diameter. Cut as you would a pie, into 8 equal wedges. Roll each piece from the wide end to the point. Bend them into slightly crescent shapes.

Let rise about 15 minutes. Brush with milk or beaten egg and bake in the middle of the oven.

Sweet Dough

This dough is the basis for many kinds of baked goods. Sweet buns, *julekake* (Christmas stollen), coffee ring, wheat cake, shilling buns – all typically Norwegian and often served at birthday celebrations for both children and adults. Makes 24 sweet buns, or 30 shilling buns, or 2 wheat cakes, or 2 Christmas stollen, or 1 coffee ring.

Ingredients
50 g/1 ½ oz yeast
3 ½ dl/1 ¼ cup/1 ½ cup milk
100–200 g/3 ½–7 oz/½–1 cup butter
100–150 g/3 ½–5 oz/½–¾ cup sugar
1 tsp cardamom
approx. ½ kg/1 lb white flour

Oven temperature:
  225–250 °C/435–480 °
Baking time: 8–35 minutes

Stir yeast into luke-warm milk, add melted butter, sugar, cardamom and enough flour to make a workable dough.

Cover dough and let rise in a warm place for about 45 minutes.

Sweet Buns
Boller

Make the dough with the least amount of butter and sugar. Divide into 24 equal parts and shape into completely round and smooth balls. Let rise again for 15 minutes. Brush with beaten egg and bake in middle of oven at highest temperature for shortest amount of time, as indicated above. The buns should be golden brown on top with a pale ring at the bottom edge.

On Shrove Sunday sweet buns are made with a little more butter than usual and are served as dessert, cut in two, filled with whipped cream and sprinkled with powdered sugar.

In Western Norway (Vestlandet) sweet buns are also eaten on Shrove Monday but are baked twice as large (divide dough into 12 parts) and flattened a little before baking. They are served in a soup dish with warm milk enriched with a large spoonful of butter and flavored with a little cardamom or cinnamon. They are called *hetevegger* or «hot walls».

Shilling Buns
Skillingsboller

Make dough with least amount of butter and sugar. Roll out into a rectangle. Brush with luke-warm water and sprinkle with a mixture of 3 Tb sugar and 2–3 tsp cinnamon. Roll the rectangle together and cut it into approx. 1 ½ cm/¾ inch slices. Let rise again and bake in middle of oven at lowest temperature for about 15 minutes.

Wheat Cake

Hvetekake

Make dough with just half of the least amount of sugar and butter. Divide dough in two and shape into round or oval loaves. Let rise again for about 15 minutes. With a sharp knife cut a cross in the top. Brush with milk or beaten egg and sprinkle with a little coarse sugar. Bake on lowest rack in the oven for approx. 25 minutes. Wheat cake is eaten with butter and cheese.

Christmas Stollen

Julekake (photo on page 76)

Make dough with largest amounts of butter and sugar. Add 2 ½ dl/1 cup/1 heaping cup raisins and 3–4 Tb candied citrus peel. When risen, divide dough in two and shape round loaves on a baking sheet or put them into bread tins. Let rise again and bake on bottom rack of oven at lowest temperature indicated for about 35 minutes. Allow a little longer baking time if loaves are baked in tins. Christmas stollen may be eaten with or without butter and is good with *geitost* (brown goat cheese).

Coffee Ring

Kringle (photo on page 76)

Make dough with largest amount of butter and smallest amount of sugar. Roll dough into a sausage, about 1 meter/1 yard long. Flatten with rolling pin so it is 10–15 cm/ 4–6 inches wide. Along the middle, spread a strip of jam or applesauce or a filling made of 100 g/3 ½ oz/½ cup of ground almonds, 6 Tb sugar and 1 egg white beaten together.

Fold dough together over filling and shape in a ring on a greased baking sheet.

Let coffee ring rise about 15 minutes. Brush with beaten egg and sprinkle with 2 Tb coarse sugar and 2 Tb chopped almonds.

Bake in the middle of the oven at lowest temperature for 25–30 minutes.

Sister Cake

Søsterkake

This delicious variant of Christmas stollen is eaten in Southern Norway (Sørlandet) on special holidays. Very rich, it is made with many eggs which gives it its fine golden color.

Ingredients
50 g/1 ¾ oz yeast
2 ½ dl/1 scant cup/1 cup milk
6 eggs
2 Tb sugar
approx. ½ kg/1 lb white flour
300 g/1 heaping cup/1 ⅓ cups butter
6 Tb raisins
4 Tb candied sitrus peel

Oven temperature: 225 °C/435 °F
Baking time: approx. 40 minutes

Stir yeast into luke-warm milk. Add eggs, sugar and flour and knead dough until smooth and elastic. Cover well and place in a warm place to rise for about 45 minutes.

Blend butter until soft and add raisins and candied peel. Knead into the risen dough.

Divide dough in two. Shape into two smooth loaves and put them in greased bread tins. Let rise again for 20–25 minutes. Brush with egg and bake in lower half of oven.

Sister cake may be eaten with or without butter.

Malt Bread

Vørterbrød (photo on page 76)

This bread is always eaten with smoked mutton (see page 39) but is also good with boiled ham and with cheese, particularly that truly Norwegian cheese, geitost.

Malt or *vørter* beer, used in the dough, is without alcohol, sweet and dark with an aromatic flavor. Other strongly flavored dark beers may be substituted.

Ingredients
50 g/1 ¾ oz yeast
1 large bottle (7 dl/just under 3 cups)
  vørter or other strongly
  flavored beer
1 tsp salt
1–1 ½ tsp anise
½ tsp pepper
½ tsp clove
7–8 Tb dark syrup
1 cup raisins
½ kg/1 lb fine rye flour
approx. ½ kg/1 lb white flour

Oven temperature: 190 °C/375 °F
Baking time: approx. 45 minutes

Heat beer carefully to lukewarm. Dissolve yeast in beer. Add remaining ingredients, reserving some of the white flour for kneading. Knead until quite firm and smooth. Cover well and let rise in a warm place at least 1 hour.

Knead dough again and divide into two equal parts. Shape round or oval loaves.

Let rise again and bake in bottom half of oven. Brush loaves with coffee or water with a little sugar added, as they are taken out of the oven. This will give the loaves a glazed crust.

Rusks

Skonroker or *kavringer*

Crunchy, crisp rusks, both sweet and un-sweetened, are found in many forms. Eaten for breakfast, lunch, before bedtime snacks and even with after-dinner coffee, they are spread with butter and cheese.

Rusks may be made with light or dark flour, but the rye rusks from Bergen de-scribed below are undoubtedly the best.

Ingredients
50 g/1 ¾ oz yeast
½ liter/1 pint water

1 tsp salt
5 Tb butter or lard
½ kg/1 lb rye flour
approx. 250 g/½ lb white flour

Oven temperature: 200 °C/390 °F
Baking time: approx. 15 minutes
Drying temperature:
  approx. 90 °C/195 °F
Drying time: 2–4 hours

Dissolve yeast in luke-warm water and add remaining ingredients. Knead dough well so it is smooth and elastic. Cover and let rise in a warm place for about 45 minutes.

Knead dough again, divide into 30 equal parts and roll into smooth, seamless balls. Bake in middle of oven. Do not let them get too brown.

Cool and cut them in half horizontally with a sharp knife.

Dry rusks until they are very light and crisp. They will keep a long while if stored in a tightly covered container.

Cream Layer Cake (Soft Cake)

Bløtkake (photo on page 77)

Cream layer cakes may be decorated and filled in many different ways. They are often filled with whipped cream and fruit or berries and completely covered with whipped cream. They may also be filled with vanilla sauce (see page 72) and deco-rated with whipped cream or powdered sugar and water icing flavored, now and then, with cocoa. Still another possibility is to fill the cake with whipped cream mixed with ground walnuts and cover top and sides with a layer of marzipan, rolled thin and topped with walnut halves. Let your imagination run rampant. Only the light sponge cake base is the same in all varia-tions.

Candles decorate the cake at birthdays, making a cheerful focal point for the birth-day table.

Ingredients
Sponge cake – about 22 cm/9 inches
in diameter
3 eggs
6 Tb sugar
6 Tb flour
3 ½ Tb potato flour or cornstarch
½ tsp baking powder

Oven temperature: 160 °C/320 °F
Baking time: 40–45 minutes

Filling 1
½ liter/1 pint heavy cream
½ liter/1 pint fresh berries, for example
raspberries or strawberries

Filling 2
2 ½ dl/1 scant cup/1 cup heavy cream
6–8 Tb ground walnuts
250 g/½ lb marzipan
halved walnut meats

Filling 3
2 portions of vanilla sauce
(see page 72)

Icing
1 cup powdered sugar
1–2 Tb cocoa
coffee or water

The cake
Beat eggs and sugar well until the mixture stands in stiff peaks – approx. 7–10 minutes with an electric beater. Too little beating will result in a fallen cake. Mix dry ingredients and fold them lightly into egg mixture.

Pour batter into a deep, greased cake tin, preferably one with a removable rim. Bake in lower half of oven until golden brown, well risen and baked through. Cool on a rack.

Slice cake in two, horizontally, and drench it with a little fruit juice, liqueur or sherry. This makes the cake extra moist and enhances its flavor.

Filling 1
Clean berries and sprinkle with sugar. Beat cream stiff. Spread half of the berries and half of the cream on lower half of cake. Spread rest of cream over top and sides of cake and garnish with remaining berries.

Filling 2
Beat cream stiff and flavor with ground walnuts and a little sugar, if desired. Spread on bottom half of cake. Roll out marzipan to a thin circle large enough to cover the whole cake. Drape it carefully over the cake, trim edges and garnish with halved walnut meats.

Filling 3
Spread cooled custard cream on bottom half of cake. Mix powdered sugar, cocoa and liquid together to a thick creamy icing. Spread over top and sides of cake. The cake may be sprinkled with sliced almonds if desired.

Mother Monsen
Mor Monsen (photo on page 77)

There are many theories about just who the lady was who gave her name to this cake. Cake-wise she must have been, in any case, for her cake is delicious.

Ingredients
375 g/12 ½ oz/1 ½ cups butter
375 g/12 ½ oz/1 ¾ cups sugar
1 Tb vanilla sugar or 1 tsp vanilla extract
8 eggs
375 g/12 ½ oz/a heaping 2 ½ cups flour
1 tsp baking powder
4 Tb currants
6 Tb chopped almonds
3 Tb coarse sugar

Oven temperature: 180 °C/355 °F
Baking time: 35–40 minutes

Cream butter and sugar light and airy. Add vanilla. Separate eggs and add egg yolks, one at a time, alternately with dry ingredients. Whip egg whites stiff and fold them into the batter.

Grease a flat cake tin, about 35 × 35 cm/14 × 14 inches and line with paper. Pour batter into tin and smooth the surface. Sprinkle with currants, almonds and sugar.

Bake in middle of the oven. Cool and cut into elongated diamonds.

Macaroon Wreath Cake

Kransekake (photo on page 78)

This beautifully decorated wreath cake is a must at every confirmation and wedding. Many bake it also at Christmas.

A good wreath cake should be a bit moist and chewy. This is something of an art to achieve, but not impossible.

It is easiest to bake the cake in special «kransekake» molds – rings in graduated sizes. If one does not have these rings, however, one can roll the dough into finger thick ropes, cut them to size and curl them into rings. The smallest rope should be 14 cm/5 ½ inches long, the next 2 cm/just under 1 inch longer and so on. Makes 18 rings.

Ingredients
500 g/1 lb almonds
500 g/1 lb powdered sugar
3 Tb flour
3 egg whites

Oven temperature: 200 °C/395 °F
Baking time: in molds, approx. 10 minutes, on baking sheet without molds, approx. 8 minutes

The cake may be made with blanched or unblanched almonds or with a mixture of the two. Made with blanched almonds, the rings have a pale golden color. Made with unblanched, the cake is darker but has a stronger flavor.

Grind almonds in a nut grinder, not in a blender. Mix them with the powdered sugar and flour, add the half-beaten egg whites. Knead dough well, using a mixmaster if desired. The dough should be quite firm but soft and easy to handle.

Grease ring molds very thoroughly and dust with semolina or farina. Roll dough into ropes, as described above, and place them in molds or cut and shape as described. Smooth spliced ends so there is no seam.

Bake in middle of oven until golden. Cool quickly, preferably in front of an open window. Brush off loose semolina.

Stack rings in a graduated tower. To steady the tower the rings may be «glued» together with a little caramelized sugar.

Wreath cake keeps well. It should be stored in a tightly covered tin. A heel of fresh bread or a raw, peeled potato stored in the tin with the cake will give it the proper chewy consistency.

It is a good idea to freeze wreath cake. Defrosted in its container it will acquire the desired chewiness.

Wreath cake may be decorated with colored paper snappers and small flags, and at weddings a miniature bride and groom are often placed on top of the tower.

To serve the cake lift the top part of the tower carefully off, remove and eat the bottom rings first, thus keeping the tower intact.

Wreath cake dough may also be rolled and baked in short sticks and served with various desserts such as ice cream, Bavarian creams and cold puddings.

Royal Cake

Fyrstekake

This is one of the most typical Norwegian cakes. It is served at coffeetime as a special treat. The cake keeps very well and is easy to make.

Ingredients
125 g/4 oz/a scant ½ cup butter
5 Tb sugar
2 egg yolks
2 Tb cold water

1 tsp baking powder
250 g/8 oz/1 ¾ cups flour

Filling
2 ½ dl/1 scant cup/1 cup almonds
150 g/1 scant cup/1 cup powdered sugar
2 egg whites

Oven temperature: 190 °C/375 °F
Baking time: 30–40 minutes

Cream butter and sugar light and airy. Add egg yolks, water and dry ingredients. Line a round cake tin, approc. 22 cm/9 inches in diameter with ⅔ of the dough.

Grind almonds and mix them with powdered sugar and egg whites. Pour mixture into dough-lined pan.

Roll remaining dough into thin ropes and lay in a lattice on top of filling. Brush, if desired, with beaten egg. Bake cake in bottom half of oven.

Cross Macaroons

Korsmakroner

These delicious little cakes have become extremely easy to make now that one can buy frozen pastry.

Ingredients
approx. 300 g/10 oz frozen pastry
2 ½ dl/1 scant cup/1 cup almonds
2 ½ dl/1 scant cup/1 cup powdered sugar
2–3 egg whites

Oven temperature: 200 °C/390 °F
Baking time: 15–18 minutes

Defrost pastry according to instructions on package. Roll it out and line 16 sand tart molds or muffin tins with it. Refrigerate.

Grind almonds and mix them with powdered sugar and egg whites.

Divide filling among pastry-lined molds. Cut remaining pastry in narrow strips and place in a cross on each cake. Brush with beaten egg white.

Bake golden brown on a baking sheet in middle of oven.

Berlin Wreaths

Berlinerkranser

One of the most popular of the traditional Christmas cookies, they are sometimes also used as an accompaniment to an elegant dessert.

Ingredients
yolks of 2 hard-boiled eggs
2 raw egg yolks
8 Tb sugar
300–350 g/10–12 oz/approx.
  2 cups flour
250 g/8 ½ oz/1 heaping cup butter

Garnish
2 egg whites
coarse sugar

Oven temperature: 180 °C/355 °F
Baking time: approx. 10 minutes

Mash hard-boiled egg yolk with a fork, add raw yolks and beat with sugar until light and fluffy.

Alternately add flour and softened butter. Handle dough as little as possible.

Roll dough into pencil thick ropes. Cut into 14 cm/5 ½ inch lengths. Shape into rings.

Dip rings first in lightly beaten egg white, then in coarse sugar.

Bake golden brown in middle of the oven.

Stacks of Planks

Bordstabelbakkels

These cakes owe their name to the fact that they are stacked on the cake platter like planks in a lumber yard.

Ingredients
2 eggs
250 g/8 ½ oz/1 cup + 2 Tb sugar
2 Tb cream
approx. 500 g/16 ½ oz/3 ½ cups flour
250 g/8 ½ oz/1 heaping cup butter

Garnish
3 egg whites
4 Tb sugar
125 g/4 1/2 oz/3/4 cup almonds

Oven temperature: 180 °C/355 °F
Baking time: approx. 10 minutes

Beat eggs and sugar light and fluffy. Add cream. Add flour and butter alternately. Chill dough at least 1 hour. It may be made a day in advance and refrigerated overnight.

Half beat egg whites, add sugar and ground almonds.

Roll dough thin and cut in rectangles about 2 1/2 × 12 cm/1 × 5 inches.

Put a strip of almond mixture down the middle of each cake. Bake cakes crisp and golden brown in middle of oven.

Sand Tarts
Sandkaker

These cakes, made in special fluted molds, may be served as other cakes with after-dinner coffee, or they may be filled with cream and fruit, for example with cloudberry cream (see page 74), and served as dessert.

Ingredients
200 g/6 1/2 oz/3/4 cup butter
10 1/2 Tb sugar
1 egg
80 g/2 1/2 oz/1/2 cup almonds
approx. 350 g/12 oz/2 cups flour
1/4 tsp baking powder

Oven temperature: 185 °C/365 °F
Baking time: approx. 20 minutes

Cream sugar and butter light and fluffy. Add egg, ground almonds and dry ingredients.

Press pieces of dough along bottom and sides of well-greased sand tart molds.

Put molds on a baking sheet in lower half of oven. Bake golden brown.

Cool on a rack. Turn upside-down and tap with back of a knife to loosen cakes from molds.

Syrup Snaps
Sirupsnipper

In Bergen these cakes are called «speculations». The word undoubtedly came from the Netherlands or northern Germany with merchants who arrived in Bergen in great numbers as early as the 15th century.

Ingredients
6 Tb dark syrup
125 g/4 1/2 oz/1/2 cup butter
2 small eggs
8 1/2 Tb sugar
2 Tb milk
approx. 400 g/13 1/2 oz/2 3/4 cups flour
3/4 tsp pepper
3/4 tsp clove
3/4 tsp ginger
1 tsp cinnamon
2 tsp grated lemon peel
2 tsp baking powder

Garnish
blanched almonds, halved

Oven temperature: 180 °C/355 °F
Baking time: 5–6 minutes

Heat syrup until liquid. Remove pan from heat and add butter. Stir until melted. Beat egg and sugar and add to syrup with milk, flour, spices and baking powder. The dough should be relatively moist. Refrigerate, over night if convenient.

Knead dough lightly and roll out thin. Cut it into diamonds or cut out figures with cooky cutters – boys, girls, Christmas trees, hearts, stars, etc.

Put half a blanched almond on each diamond.

Bake cookies in middle of oven until evenly brown and crisp.

Goro

Baked on a special iron, goro is one of our oldest cakes. Today, we may use either an iron that is heated on top of the stove or an electric iron. In former times, irons of this sort were very heavy with long handles to allow them to be used over the open fire. But now, as then, they are beautifully decorated with a pattern of flowers and leaves.

Ingredients
1 egg
6 Tb sugar
6 Tb heavy cream
1 Tb cognac
grated peel of ½ lemon
½ tsp cardamom
250 g/8 ½ oz/1 heaping cup butter
4 Tb potato flour or cornstarch
approx. 300 g/10 oz/2 cups flour

Beat egg and sugar light and fluffy.
  Beat cream stiff. Add to egg mixture with cognac and spices.
  Stir in a little flour, melted butter and remaining flour. The dough should be quite thin.
  Cover well and refrigerate over night.
  Cut a paper pattern the exact size of the iron. Roll out dough and cut it the same size as the pattern.
  Put cakes on the iron and bake on both sides on top of stove. In an electric iron both sides are baked at once. The cakes should be a delicate pale yellow. Trim edges while cakes are warm.

Curled Cookies

Krumkaker

Unlike the rectangular *goro* iron, the *krumkake* iron is round. It, too, is beautifully decorated. The cookies get their characteristic shape by being curled around a wooden cone. Both the iron, electric or heated on top of the stove, and the wooden cone may be purchased throughout the country. Curled cookies may also be draped in a cup and later filled with fruit and whipped cream, for example cloudberry cream (see page 74) or ice cream, and served as dessert.

Ingredients
12 Tb sugar
200 g/6 ½ oz/¾ cup butter
4 eggs
1 tsp cardamom
approx. 250 g/8 ½ oz/1 ¾ cups flour
3–4 Tb cold water

Cream sugar and butter light and airy.
  Add eggs, one at a time, alternately with flour and cardamom, mixed. Add water.
  Pour a spoonful of batter on iron, press it shut and bake cookies golden on each side (the electric iron bakes both sides at once).
  Curl them around the wooden cone or in a cup while they are warm.

Strull

These cakes may be made in the *krumkake* iron, but they should be rolled into a thin, even roll, for example around the handle of a wooden spoon.

Ingredients
2 dl/¾ cup/a heaping ¾ cup sour cream
3 Tb cold water
4 Tb sugar
100 g/3 ½ oz/10 Tb flour

Beat sour cream stiff with the sugar and add the water. Fold in flour.
  Bake as for curled cookies. Roll them while they are warm.

Avletter

(photo on page 95)

These delicious cakes are among the very oldest known. They are baked in a beautifully decorated *avlett* iron or in a *krumkake* iron, but, unlike *krumkaker* they are not curled but left flat.

Ingredients

½ liter/1 pint heavy cream
¼ liter/1 seant cup/1 cup sour cream
4 dl/1 ⅓ cup/1 ½ cup water
¼ tsp salt
2 tsp sugar
approx. 400 g/13 ½ oz/2 ¾ cups flour

Beat all ingredients to a smooth batter with the consistency of pancake batter. Bake thin cakes in the *avlett* or *krumkake* iron. Serve them plain or with sour cream or whipped cream and fresh berries.

Sour Cream Waffles

Rømmevafler (photo on page 95)

We eat a lot of waffles in Norway. Simple, inexpensive waffles for every day, finer waffles for special occasions. And sour cream waffles are absolutely something special. Crisp and warm, eat them with *geitost* or jam and, for a treat, with a spoonful of sour cream.

Ingredients

½ liter/1 pint rich sour cream
6–8 Tb water
175 g/6 oz/1 ¼ cups flour
1 tsp salt
1 tsp baking powder

Mix all ingredients to a smooth batter and let it stand and swell for 5–10 minutes. Bake the waffles over relatively low heat in an electric waffle iron or one that is heated over the stove. They should be crisp and golden brown.

Poor Man

Fattigmann

No one has been able to explain just why these cookies, which are anything but inexpensive to make, should be called «poor man». One theory is that one becomes poor buying the ingredients to bake them. It is not hard to believe this when onc realizes that our grandmothers' recipe for poor

man called for 30 eggs. But there were many more mouths to feed in those days.

Ingredients

4 egg yolks
1 whole egg
4 Tb sugar
3 Tb heavy cream
1 Tb cognac
½ tsp grated lemon peel
½ tsp cardamom
approx. 180 g/6 oz/1 ¼ cups flour

Beat egg yolks, egg and sugar light and fluffy. Beat cream stiff and add it to egg mixture with cognac. Add spices and flour. The dough should be somewhat moist. Cover well and refrigerate over night.

Roll dough thin and cut in diamonds. Cut a lengthwise incision in the middle of each diamond and pull one pointed end of the cooky through the cut to give the cookies their characteristic shape.

Bake golden brown in deep fat or oil for 2–3 minutes. Cool on absorbent paper.

Stag's Antlers

Hjortetakk

Many say that it isn't really Christmas unless the house smells of deep-fat frying. Aside from poor man, stag's antlers are the most usual deep-fried cake.

Cakes fried in deep-fat have traditions that go back to the days before masonry ovens were common in the home.

Ingredients

3 eggs
180 g/12 Tb sugar
6 Tb heavy cream
5 Tb melted butter
2 Tb cognac
grated peel of ½ lemon
½ tsp cardamom
approx. 450 g/15 oz/3 ¼ cups flour

Beat egg and sugar light. Add cream, whipped, melted butter, cognac and spices and stir in flour. Refrigerate dough over night.

Knead dough lightly adding a little more flour if necessary, but the cakes are best if as little flour as possible is used.

Roll dough into pencil thick ropes and cut into 10 cm/4 inches lengths. Shape into rings and cut 4–5 incisions in each. Fry golden brown in deep fat or oil. Drain well on absorbent paper.

Rosettes

Rosettbakkels (photo on page 75)

In the region around the town of Røros, these cakes are called lace cookies. That is how light and thin they should be. They are served with the finest cloudberries at Christmas. A special iron is used to make these cakes which are fried in deep fat.

Ingredients
9 Tb flour
2 Tb sugar
3 small eggs
12 Tb milk

Beat all ingredients to a smooth batter. Let is stand and swell a few minutes.

Dip the rosette iron into the hot fat. Shake off extra fat and dip the iron into the cake batter. Dip the iron into the fat again and fry cakes golden brown.

Drain on absorbent paper.

Sour Cream Cakes

Rømmebrød

These unusual cakes are made differently in different parts of the country. This recipe comes from Hallingdal, where the cakes are stacked in large piles on a stemmed cake platter decorated with traditional Norwegian rosepainting.

Ingredients
½ liter/1 pint sour cream
½ kg/1 lb butter
250 g/8 ½ oz/1 heaping cup lard
2 Tb light syrup
approx. 1 kg/2 lb flour

Mix together sour cream, softened butter, lard and syrup. Add enough flour to make a firm dough.

Roll dough thin – the thinner the dough, the better the cakes. Fry the cakes on a *takke*, griddle or frying pan.

Sprinkle sugar on cakes as they are fried and fold them at once into triangles.

Break off pieces of the cakes to serve.

Flat Bread

Flatbrød

This is assumed to be the oldest form of bread in Norway. Traditionally *flatbrød* was baked twice a year in quantities large enough to insure an adequate supply of bread for half a year. For everyday use *flatbrød* was somewhat thick and made of coarsely milled flour. For special occasions it was made of finer flour and baked paper-thin, but either way the bread was dry and crisp. It was made with or without potatoes and with various flour combinations. *Flatbrød* accompanied all kinds of food, soup, fish and meat, and was also eaten crushed in a bowl with milk poured over – a little like cornflakes. At Christmas time it was used in *mølje*, a dish of *flatbrød* covered with the greasy stock from boiled Christmas meats.

Flatbrød is eaten even today as an accompaniment to several kinds of food.

Ingredients
250 g/8 oz/1 ¾ cups barley flour or
oat flour
250 g/8 oz/1 ¾ cups coarsely or
finely milled whole wheat flour
250 g/8 oz/1 ¾ cups fine rye flour
¾ tsp salt
½ liter/1 pint skimmed milk

Combine flours and salt and make a hole in the middle. Pour in milk and stir well. Knead to a smooth elastic dough.

Divide into equal amounts and roll into round sheets, preferably with a grooved rolling pin specially designed for making *flatbrød*. Fry on both sides on a dry *takke*, griddle of frying pan. Made on a *flatbrød takke*, 45 cm/18 inches in diameter this recipe will make approx. 10–12 *flatbrød* wafers. Griddles or frying pans with smaller diameters make proportionately more. Cool on a rack and stack in piles with a weight on top. *Flatbrød* keeps a long while if stored dry.

Lompe

(Photo on page 95)

Children all consider hot dogs with *lompe* a special treat, grown ups too, for that matter. They are sold from street stands throughout the country. *Lompe* is a simple unyeasted bread patty made from potatoes and flour. Available in all grocery stores, it is also very easily made at home.

As well as being eaten with hot dogs, *lompe* accompanies cured and dried meats and is also eaten spread with butter and *geitost* (brown goat cheese). When made extra large, lompe is known as potato *lefse*.

Ingredients
1 kg/2 lb potatoes
1 tsp salt
approx. 200 g/6 ½ oz/1 ½ cups flour

Boil potatoes in their peels. Peel and mash them with the salt while they are warm.

Knead mashed potatoes with flour. The less flour used, the better the *lompe*. Roll dough into a long sausage and divide into equal pieces. With rolling pin roll into round sheets, approx. ¼ cm/⅛ inch thick. Fry on a hot, dry griddle or frying pan.

Lefse

(Photo on page 56)

Lefse is another flat unleavened bread with traditions that go back hundreds of years. As in the case of *flatbrød, lefse* was made with dark coarsely milled flour and baked thicker and more filling for everyday use, with finely milled flour for special occasions and holidays.

Lefse varies from region to region so that it can not be claimed that any one recipe is typical for the whole country.

Most *lefse* is fried on a *takke* or griddle. Some are fried dry and crisp and are later softened in water before serving.

Lefse may be served with butter and sugar or cheese; with a special spread made of butter; sour cream; sugar and cinnamon; with a cheese spread made by boiling milk to the color of caramel *(gomme)*; or in several other ways.

In some places *lefse* is rolled around cured fish, lye fish or head cheese. Every community has its customs.

The soft *lefse* recipe given here is simple to make. They should be baked in the oven and eaten with butter and sugar or cheese.

Ingredients
2 dl/¾ cup/a heaping ¾ cup sour cream
2 dl/¾ cup/a heaping ¾ cup kefir
  or buttermilk
3 Tb syrup
3 Tb sugar
3 tsp baking powder
ca ½ kg/1 lb flour

Oven temperature: 230 °C/445 °F
Baking time: 5–7 minutes

Beat together cream, milk, syrup and sugar. Add flour and baking powder, mixed. Mix dough lightly. It should be moist.

Knead dough lightly on counter and roll into a sausage.

Divide into 6 equal portions and roll to round sheets approx. 25 cm/10 inches in diameter. Prick them well with a fork and bake quickly in the middle of the oven.

Page 95
Old-fashioned baked goods are still just as popular. Above: sour cream waffles (recipe on page 92), and *lompe* (recipe on page 94). Below: *avletter* (recipe on page 91).

94

Open-faced Sandwiches

Smørbrød (photo on page 96)

Bread spread with butter and covered with some sort of topping is eaten by Norwegians at practically any time of day and on any occasion.

Open-faced sandwiches are basic breakfast food, and a true Norwegian always brings a packaged lunch consisting of open-faced sandwiches to school or work. He also serves them to his guests.

Sandwich spreads for everyday meals are simple – herring, cured meats, liver paté, cod roe caviar, goat cheese, yellow cheese and other tasty spreads that wrap well.

For guests, however, they are more elegantly prepared with plenty of the most expensive varieties of topping. Smoked salmon, lobster, shrimp, ham, roast beef and soft cheeses, attractively garnished with lemon, pickles, nuts, aspic, olives, etc. Party sandwiches are also smaller than those eaten every day and are called *snitter* or wedges.

As a tourist in a Norwegian restaurant at midday you may be surprised to see that everyone is eating open-faced sandwiches and drinking coffee or tea.

At late suppers, a common way of entertaining in Norway, the sandwiches are accompanied by beer and, now and then, a dram of aquavit, while white wine is drunk with sandwiches at midday receptions, as, for example, christenings.

A meal of open-sandwiches is very often finished off with an extra good cake and a cup of coffee.

Here are some of the most popular open-faced sandwiches:

Page 96
Top: Appetizing sandwiches with tasty spreads are good both for lunch and supper (recipes on page 97–98)

Bottom: A tempting cheese platter with Norwegian produced cheeses (see page 99). Clockwise from left: *Norzola,* a Norwegian variety of roquefort; *gamalost,* the most Norwegian of all Norwegian cheeses; *Jarlsberg,* a cheese which is in great demand in many parts of the world; a flavored cream cheese resembling the French *boursin;* and Norwegian *camembert.*

Anchovics and Egg Sandwich

Butter dark bread and cover it with slices of hardboiled egg. Top with two fillets of anchovies. Garnish with fresh dill.

Sardine Sandwich

Butter whole wheat bread and cover with slices of tomatoes. Sprinkel a little salt and pepper over the tomatoes. Place three sardines on the tomatoes and garnish with parsley.

Herring with Raw Egg Yolk

Butter dark bread and place anchovy fillets or marinated herring pieces *(gaffelbiter)* in a circle on top. Garnish with chopped raw onion, pickles and pickled beets and place a raw egg yolk in the center.

Shellfish Sandwich

Butter white bread and place a leaf of lettuce on it. Cover with a pile of shrimp, or crab or lobster meat from the claws. Garnish with mayonnaise, lemon and dill.

Liver Paté Sandwich

Butter *kneipp* or whole wheat bread. Cover with a slice of liver paté and garnish with crisp fried bacon, fried mushrooms and pickles.

Smoked or Cured Salmon/Sea Trout Sandwich

Butter white bread and place a leaf of lettuce on it. Cover with a spoonful of cooled scrambled eggs and a large slice of smoked or cured fish. Garnish with dill.

Ham Sandwich

Butter *kneipp* or whole wheat bread and cover with Italian salad (cooked carrot and celeriac, raw apple and cabbage, pickles and ham, all chopped and mixed with mayonnaise). Roll 2–3 thin ham slices around boiled asparagus tips and place on salad.

Cured Ham Sandwich

Butter dark bread and cover with thin slices of cured ham. Put a big spoonful of cooled scrambled eggs on top and garnish with sliced cucumber.

Roast Beef Sandwich

Butter white bread and cover with 5–6 thin slices of roast beef. Garnish with a spoonful of remoulade and finely chopped dark aspic.

Beef Tartar Sandwich

Butter dark bread and cover with a patty of freshly ground or scraped tender raw beef. Press a hollow in the middle of the patty and place a raw egg yolk in the hollow. Garnish with finely chopped onion, capers, chopped pickles and chopped pickled beets.

Cheese Sandwich

Butter white bread and cover with thick slices of Jarlsberg cheese cut into triangles. Garnish with thinly sliced radish and pickle.

Gamalost (Old Cheese) Sandwich

Butter dark bread and cover with a paper-thin slice of *gamalost*. Garnish with butter balls that are spread over the cheese before eating.

Goat Cheese Snack

This is a sandwich made from cheese only – without bread. It is a way of eating cheese which has long traditions in Norway. Cut thick slices of white goat cheese. Butter and cover with slices of brown goat cheese.

Fruit Sandwich

Butter white bread and sprinkle with finely chopped parsley. Place a thick slice of apple, lightly boiled, on the bread. Fill the middle of the apple with red currant marmalade.

Some Slices of Cheese

Ost (photo on page 96)

Cheese has never been used in Norway as it is in the rest of Europe. It is usually eaten on bread for breakfast, lunch, or in-between-meal snacks, and is always found on the traditional *smørgåsbord* or buffet table.

Cheese is popular in Norway, and a wide variety of imported and domestic cheeses are to be found in food stores throughout the country.

Norway alone produces around 60 different kinds of cheese, some of them typically Norwegian, others inspired by cheeses from other countries. Thus, one may buy a domestic Swiss, Gouda, Edamer, Cheddar etc. Many of these cheeses have been given Norwegian names. For instance, domestic Gouda, the most popular cheese in Norway today, has been renamed Norvegia. It is made – as are several other cheeses – both with a rind and rind free. A low fat variety, called Vega, is also produced.

Swiss cheese arrived in Norway over 150 years ago, with Swiss who came to the country for various reasons. This cheese has had a great influence on Norwegian dairy product development.

Swiss cheese was made many places in Norway, among others at the Jarlsberg Estates near Tønsberg. It was, at the Jarlsberg dairy, moreover, that a special cheese with a distinctive flavor was developed, highly prized from its inception at the beginning of the last century. Increased import of cheese from Holland, unfortunately, forced the Jarlsberg dairy to discontinue production of this excellent cheese. It was not forgotten, however, and early in the 1960's production was renewed. Today Jarlsberg cheese is in great demand, not only in Norway, but throughout the world. The United States provides one of the largest markets.

Aside from Jarlsberg, Norway exports large quantities of Norvegia, *Nøkkelost* (key cheese) and Gudbrandsdalsost, as well as lesser amounts of other cheeses. Our biggest customers are the United States, Sweden, Australia and Japan.

Gamalost, literally, «old» cheese, has been made for centuries. Indigenous to Norway, it is not found any place else in the world. It is a low fat cheese, made of soured skim milk and left to mature for only 5 weeks before it is sent on to the market. *Gamalost* has a characteristic tangy flavor, an unusual brownish color and a dry, soft, granular consistency. It is eaten on dark bread or rye crisp with butter spread under and over the cheese.

Pultost, a soft, caraway flavored cheese, was formerly home-made on the farms, much as cottage cheese. It is produced from clabbered milk, stirred and heated until the curd separates from the whey. The curd is then crumbled or ground and flavored with salt and caraway. It must then be matured for three or four weeks before it is ready to eat.

Geitost, or goat cheese, is considered by many to be the most typically Norwegian cheese. This rectangular, brown «brick» is really not a cheese at all, as it is made from the whey after it is separated from the curds. *Geitost* is found on every Norwegian breakfast table and is a customary element in the lunch box. There are different grades of *geitost*.

Gudbrandsdalsost is the most popular type of *geitost*. It is a «hybrid», made of a mixture of goat and cow milk, and gets its name from the fact that it was first made in Gudbrandsdal, a long fertile valley in central Norway. *Gudbrandsdalsost* is now produced in dairies all over the country.

True, pure *geitost* is made from 100 % goat whey, milk, and cream. It has a far stronger flavor than *Gudbrandsdalsost*.

In former times goat cheese was boiled in iron kettles that left traces of natural iron in the finished product. Modern production methods have deprived goat cheese of its iron content. To compensate for this, 10 mg of liquid iron sulfate is now added to every 100 gr of *geitost*.

What do Norwegians Drink?

Norway is one of the few countries in the world where it is quite natural to drink fresh, cold milk at breakfast – not only the children, but also the adults drink milk. The milk may be sweet or soured, skimmed or whole, but the milk glass belongs on the breakfast table.

One is also bound to notice that coffee is a popular drink. In fact, more coffee is drunk in Norway and Finland than in any other country in the world. The average consumption is 3 cups of coffee per inhabitant per day – not so strange that coffee is said to be Norway's national drink. If you drop in on friends informally, you are immediately served a cup of coffee. If you need an invigorating drink in the course of the day, you have a cup of coffee. If you wake up in the middle of the night and can't get to sleep, you get up and drink some coffee.

On the other hand, we do not drink much tea, even though there are people, here too, who prefer tea to coffee both at breakfast and lunch.

Beer, as everyone knows, is an old, tried and true drink. For everyday purposes beer, in former times, was undoubtedly sour and thin, but it was brewed strong and flavorful for important holidays. «Beer» was, in fact, synonomous with a feast. Thus *juleøl* or «Christmas beer» was the equivalent of a Christmas celebration, *festerøl* or «engagement beer» meant an engagement party. And beer is the drink that tastes best with nearly all traditional Norwegian foods. Beer is often drunk as a chaser with aquavit which is distilled from potatoes. In Norway aquavit is not drunk ice cold, as it is other places in Europe. The flavor is at its best when the dram is served at room temperature.

Norwegians, as is well known, have always been wanderers. On their many, long journeys they have learned to appreciate the wine they sampled in foreign countries. Grapes do not grow in our harsh climate, but our foremothers taught themselves the art of making wine from berries and fruits that they grew in their own gardens or picked in the woods and fields. Wine-making is still a favorite Norwegian hobby. Wild blueberries and rose-hips picked in the woods, currants, gooseberries, apples and rhubarb from the garden, may be transformed into delicious wine that is often brought out to honor good friends. Even if the result is not always equally successful and the guest might have preferred a glass from a bottle bought at the Wine Monopoly, he makes the best of a bad bargain and praises his host's product. At large gatherings cocktails are served before dinner in the American tradition, wine with the food and cognac and liqueur with coffee in the French tradition. And the evening is concluded with highballs in the English tradition.

A Few Words about Norwegian Produce

Most of the ingredients that are used in the recipes in this book may be purchased in almost any part of the world. The exceptions are game such as ptarmigan, black grouse and capercaillie. Stock doves or pigeons may be prepared in the same way as ptarmigan and taste very similar to ptarmigan.

Some of our native berries may also be difficult to find in other countries. Cranberries, which are larger and have a thicker skin than lingonberries, may be substituted with satisfactory results. For cloudberries with their rich aroma and individual flavor it is difficult to find a substitute.

The greatest difficulty may arise in using the recipes for breads and cakes, as flour varies greatly from country to country. Here is a simplified descricption of the types of flour found in Norway:

White flour – extraction rate 78, unbleached, without additives
1 dl = 60 g, 1 Tb = 10 g
Whole wheat, coarsely milled – extraction rate 100, the whole grain is milled to flour, without additives
1 dl = 55 g 1 Tb = 9 g
Whole wheat, finely milled – extraction rate 100, the same as coarsely milled whole wheat but with finer grain
1 dl = 55 g, 1 Tb = 9 g
Rye flour, blended with 15 % white flour for improved baking results – extraction rate 70, without additives
1 dl = 60 g, 1 Tb = 10 g
Coarsely milled rye, similar to coarsely milled whole wheat
1 dl = 55 g, 1 Tb = 9 g
Finely milled rye, similar to finely milled whole wheat
1 dl = 55 g, 1 Tb = 9 g
Barley flour – extraction rate 50 or 70, a semi-fine flour with a strong flavor. It may be added in small amounts to bread dough. It is mostly used in *flatbrød* and in a few special unyeasted baked goods.
1 dl = 45 g, 1 Tb = 7 g
Potato flour – pure potato starch, used to thicken soups and sauces and in some cakes
1 dl = 70 g, 1 Tb = 12 g, 1 tsp = 4 g

For the sake of simplicity, the term butter has been used in all recipes. Margarin may, of course, be substituted. Both butter and margarin have a fat content of 81 %. Norwegian butter is pure and without additives. Margarin is enriched with vitamins A and D. Both a firm and a soft variety of margarin may be purchased.

Conversion Table for Weights and Measures

In all the recipes, ingredients are listed with their metric, English and American equivalents (in that order). When table spoons (Tb) and teaspoons (tsp) are used, the standard sized measuring spoons are assumed.

1 dl = 10 cl = 100 ml
1 Tb = 15 ml   6 Tb dry ingredients = 1 dl
   7 Tb liquid = 1 dl
1 tsp = 5 ml
1 English cup flour = 170 g
1 American cup flour = 140 g
1 English cup sugar = 255 g
1 American cup sugar = 210 g
1 English cup butter = 270 g
1 American cup butter = 225 g

To simplify the measuring process, the following approximate conversions have been used:

½ liter = 1 pint, 1 liter = 1 qt
½ kg = 1 lb
100 g = 3 ½ oz
1 oz = 30 g
1 English cup = 2 ¾ dl (2.84 dl)
1 American cup = 2 ½ dl (2.37 dl)

All recipes in this book are for 4 persons unless otherwise stated.

Index – English

Index – Norwegian